THEY CALLED HIM WHITE CHOCOLATE

Nancy Carroll McEndree

Copyright © 2021 by Nancy Carroll McEndree

ISBN   Softcover   978-1-953537-67-6

All rights reserved. No part of this book may be reproduced or transmitted in any form or by any means, electronic or mechanical, including photocopying, recording, or by any information storage and retrieval system without express written permission from the author, except in the case of brief quotations embodied in critical reviews and certain other non-commercial uses permitted by copyright law.

Printed in the United States of America.

To order additional copies of this book, contact:
Bookwhip
1-855-339-3589
www.bookwhip.com

CONTENTS

Dedication v
Acknowledgement vii
Preface - Jim Remembers.. ix

Chapter 1   Nancy's Turn to Remember 1
Chapter 2   Remembering—The Beginning 5
Chapter 3   Remembering—The Teen Age Years........................... 13
Chapter 4   Remembering the Middle and Pre-teen Years............... 20
Chapter 5   Remembering the Young Married Years 28
Chapter 6   Remembering the Second Marriage and
            Half-way House.. 34
Chapter 7   Remembering Leaving The Half Way House
            And Living on the Street.. 49
Chapter 8   Remembering Pastor Helen And Shaw University........ 53
Chapter 9   Remembering Ruby and A Life Changing Event 57
Chapter 10 Remembering Jim's Phone Call.................................... 60
Chapter 11 Remembering the Rehabilitation Experience &
            the Assault 66
Chapter 12 Remembering The Veteran's Hospital Experience
            & Senator Jenny Brown Waite..................................... 73
Chapter 13 Remembering the Last Two Happy Years..................... 80
Chapter 14 Remembering: Jim Falls Asleep.................................... 87
Chapter 15 Remembering Jim – My Concluding Thoughts 90

DEDICATION

Jim and I dedicate this book to all people who have suffered with or have lived through depression, despondency, sexual and physical abuse, misery, bitterness, heartache, poverty, and down and out hard times. I firmly believe that all who have found themselves in these circumstances can experience as Jim did, that these tragedies do not have to be the final estate and the end of any life story. We all have an escape clause! Anyone can give their ugly messed up scared life to our Heavenly Father, and He will transform scars into forgiven and redeemed Heaven bound shooting stars!

ACKNOWLEDGEMENT

My gratitude and thanks to: My Sweetheart, Duane, my husband and my life. Thank you, my darling, for supporting me in all my life endeavors. We have grown in Christ, we have dreamed, and we have known a love that God has blessed, and we will go on forever and ever and beyond!

To Charles and Terri McEndree: Thank you, my darlings, for supporting and believing in my work. Thank you for investing in the publication of this book. You are my jewels, and no diamond or ruby could shine brighter in my eyes.

To Patricia Carroll: Thank you, my Sister, for contributing information that I used in my book. I love you, and we will see Jim again when we all get to Heaven. What a blessed day that will be!

To Jim and Juliet Patterson: A very special thank you for all your prayers, your encouragement, your music, hard work, and long hours put into the design of the cover of "Remembering Jim". Daddy and I love you both so very much, and we appreciate your zealousness for the work of God and for the message of the Loud Cry to resound all over the world.

In Memoriam: Michael Carroll, thank you Mike for contributing information that I used in this book. I miss you and love you. I will look for you in Heaven.

Thanks to all my children, grandchildren, and great grandchild. Thank you for loving me and helping me navigate through the peaks and valleys of life.

PREFACE—JIM REMEMBERS

Then He Falls Asleep

Jim tells in his own words the beginning, the middle, and the ending final days of his life. He leads into my taking over the manuscript with his overview and then says —
<u>*Goodbye*</u>*!*

Anytime a person wishes to write an autobiography, there has to be ego involved. Therefore, I ask the reader to take this into consideration. Even after admitting this, I say to you, Dear Reader, that the main purpose of this narrative is to glorify God and lead others, by my testimony, to the saving grace of Almighty God. This admission leads me to pray: "Lord, God, you have given me the ability to express myself with pen and paper. I ask you to anoint each page of this manuscript, each jot and tittle, with the power to lead this lost world to your saving grace. If only one person were saved because of my meager attempts to tell my life story, then my time and effort despite my pain and fragile body are well worth the effort put forth."

One can quickly ascertain that this book does not attempt to fill every slice and detail of my life. At this time I remember and meditate on the many challenging and violent times that God was with me and saved my life. I am so thankful that when I needed My Father the most, He helped me understand that to really live, you must really die to self. That's the way it was with me!

A milestone is reached in the life of a child, when he reaches the age of accountability. This occurrence happens, for most of us, at age twelve or thirteen. But for most of us, the mind is the maturity factor and that is a whole different ball game. Immaturity, irresponsibility and selfishness can consume one into middle age as it did with me. As I look back telescopically, I can see very little value attached to my youthful years except for the fact that I grew stronger and acquired resilience. I had to thrive in a home of violence and torture meted out by a despotic father who administered punishment to me that a very thick skinned animal would have trouble surviving.

As a young virile adult man, the physical pleasures were the main menu of the day. As a youth, I learned to survive the madness of the world and now as a tall, strong, handsome hunk, I was ready for titillating action and enjoyment and no one and nothing was going to keep me from it! I had learned from my father that the biggest and strongest dominates his desires and demands on the weakest and so my agenda was wine, women, and song. Unfortunately many years of my life were devoted to this wasteful pursuit.

Before my trifling and partying was complete, I received a beautifully written letter from my "Uncle Sam". He was drafting me and sending me to Korea where I found myself in the Air Force back up team to a USA spy operation on the DMZ. Little did I know how the defoliant in those copper canisters that I helped the ROK (Republic of Korea) soldiers spray on the foliage would cripple and change my life later on.

Not only was this duty dangerous and tedious at times, but the 'party hardy' times grew more intensive. Women were plentiful and very attracted to US soldiers who would help fleece them and also their families. Anytime I wanted a woman or even a young girl, one was readily available. Booze was what we drunk at breakfast, dinner, and supper, and if you wanted street drugs, well they weren't hard to get either. My biggest concern was to stay out of trouble and get back home safely.

I did get back home but only to find the situation there worse that when I left. As I got out of the taxi and started to climb the porch stairs I saw my father, (I hadn't seen him for 4 years) and all he said to me was "Hi" and left me standing there! My mother screamed when I walked into the kitchen and was obviously very happy to see me but she had to go to work. My mother worked because she got almost no physical or financial help from my father. He abused her frequently to the point that I had feared for her life.

The hero had just returned from the war zone, and no one was there to welcome me home. I was all alone. My sister was married and lived in Wisconsin and my younger brother was seldom home because he wanted to avoid the abuse.

At age 21 I got married. At the time, it seemed the thing to do. I had more "street" experience than any 21 year old kid should have, but I really had no common "sense". My wife, Claire, and I were happy at first, but then the children came with all the responsibilities of raising a family and making a living. I was a total big, fat, failure, and I was not faithful to my wife. Claire finally had a belly full of it, we divorced and I deserted my children.

I suspect that for most people the day of their salvation is somewhere close to the youthful years of their life. For me, life truly began when middle age was fast approaching. That's when I lost everything and was born again.

In 1987 I turned 43 years of age and had a wonderful hardworking intelligent wife and three beautiful, precious children and in two weeks' time, for all intents and purposes, I lost my car, my job, my home, my children, and my wife. In one giant brushstroke, I seemingly lost it all.

In no way am I blaming God now. I brought all my woes on myself. God did, however get my attention. Some people claim that the Holy Spirit is very gentle. This I can certainly tell you, Dear Reader, if the Holy Spirit wants your attention and gentle nudging has not worked, He is not adverse to using a spiritual two by four.

I remember driving down the road from Plymouth, New Hampshire, in a borrowed car. I was crying so hard that I could barely see. I slowly pulled over to the side of the road, raised my fist skyward and shouted, "G-- d--- You, God. Then I realized that I had asked God to curse Himself. Then fear gripped me because I was encased in the terrible presence of being alone.

My next utterance was a bit more subdued. "Lord, I said, please help me. I've really fouled things up this time!"

I have no idea how long I stayed there, but I finally regained my sensibility then started the car's engine and began driving again. I must have been no more than two hundred yards further along on the road, when I saw a sign that said, 'Jesus Saves', next to the sign, stood a quaint little chapel. I stopped the car, got out of it, and walked over to the chapel. I tried to open the door and even though it was the middle of the week, to my surprise, the chapel door was unlocked. I walked inside of the building to find off in a corner of the small edifice a nondescript little old man praying.

"Come on in, young man," he said, "I've been waiting for you. Is there something you'd like to say?"

For no apparent reason I started to cry again. In response to my action this little old man that I had just met made this reply. "You don't have to say anything. The Lord has already told me all I need to know about you." Then this total stranger, in a few short minutes told me my life's story. How could he have known all of this about me? He even knew accurate details about me as a young boy hiding in the dog house in sub degree weather in winter time in New Hampshire, huddled there in fear for the beating inflicted by my father. He told me of the bull whippings that I endured and of the intense belittling and verbal bashing that I live with on a daily basis.

Finally he asked if he could pray for me. He asked me to repeat his words if I was in agreement. What he asked me to repeat is sometimes called the sinner's prayer. He asked me to acknowledge that:

1. I was a sinner.
2. I had a desire to have my sins washed away.
3. An admission that Jesus loved me and was Lord and Savior in my life.
4. To admit that I had a desire to spend eternity with Him in Heaven.

After I finished this simple prayer, I felt as if a thousand pounds were lifted from my shoulders. Many people who have experienced that moment of salvation indicate that nothing in the supernatural seemed to happen. That, however, was not the way it happened for me. I definitely felt a heavy weight lift from my body. I felt as if I floated on air as I walked outside to get into my car. I don't remember what I said to the little old man as I left the chapel and I don't ever remember meeting him again.

I was pressed for time to get to the bank for a money transaction, but I was so happy that I felt compelled to tell anyone and everyone who would listen about my recent conversion. The bank teller looked at me strangely when I told her I was saved, but that didn't squelch my enthusiasm. I was really happy, perhaps for the first time in my life. Since that day my greatest joy is to bring the salvation message to any and all, the rich and the poor, the lonely and downtrodden, the sick and the well, because God loves them all. The Bible says "for he who wins souls is wise" (Proverbs 11:30, NIV), and I've spent many hours with Jesus, fishing for men.

After I deserted my family, I reached my lowest ebb. I lived in a half-way house, on the street, in my car, and finally in the ghetto in Greensboro, North Carolina. With much help from people who recognized that I had intelligence and compassion, I enrolled at Shaw University, I was one of the first "White" graduates from that university. In fact my classmates lovingly called me "white chocolate". I went on and finished a master's program and was enrolled to work on a doctorate in divinity.

One day all the plans I had made to be one of Christ's fishermen in the ghetto and complete my education were flushed down the gutter. I was working as a hospital chaplain when I fainted four separate times while making my rounds. After many exhausting tests, the doctors diagnosed me with CLL *(chronic lymphatic leukemia)*. I was very ill.

I had not seen my sister, Nancy, for over 20 years. We were very close when we were kids. I needed help, so I called her. I told her, "Nancy, I am dying, I need your help." Nancy did not hesitate but told me to come to Florida where she and my brother-in-law, Duane, would take care of me.

For almost two years since coming to Florida, I have fought the good fight to stay alive. Every day I can feel my body getting weaker. I say little of this to Nancy, but I know that she realizes what is going on. My sister and Duane keep telling me that I will get well and they lovingly care for me, feed me, push my wheel chair (even running wheel chair races), chauffeur me to doctor and hospital appointments. The three of us have Bible study together almost every day. As my body weakens, our love for the Lord and each other grows stronger.

Nancy will finish my book. She is already a published author and she knows my story well. I know that I have a very few days left on earth and I am trying to prepare my much loved sister for my death and homecoming to live with Jesus. I have asked her to read these words at my memorial service: I will rest easy knowing that I have served the God of my ancestors. I have fought the good fight and I have finished the race. I will no longer be with you physically, but I will always be with you spiritually.

Please do not cry for me for I have gone to a better place. My work on earth has been fruitful, and it is now done, so I say to you "Death be not proud." Remember God's promises and do not be afraid. Please accept the gift of salvation. Life is for the living. I am now in the arms of the Almighty, who will never let me go. Please believe and know this because it is a promise for you also.

Good bye. God bless you. I will see you again in a little while. Don't cry too much, Nancy, even though I know you will! I LOVE YOU! "Jim"

CHAPTER ONE

Nancy's Turn to Remember

I wondered if I would recognize my brother as I watched the passengers come off the train and walk through the long corridor to retrieve their luggage. I found myself looking intently at the passengers' faces as I strained to recognize one of the men as Jim.

It had been about twenty years since I'd last seen him. My brother, Jim, had literally disappeared from the family. He had simply vanished, leaving no forwarding address or phone number. We were very close as children; my family and I were heartbroken by his decision to leave New Hampshire.

I tried to find Jim through a tracing agency, and I did find him once after a two-year search. He was living in a halfway house in North Carolina. After briefly speaking by phone with Pastor Wily, the director of the half-way house, he handed the phone to Jim. "Nancy, I left New Hampshire for many reasons, none of which I wish to discuss with you. You have your life and I have mine. Don't try to contact me again," he said. Then he hung up the phone. I was devastated.

My family and I decided that if Jim wanted no contact with us, we should respect his wishes, so I reluctantly let my brother go. I was flabbergasted when Jim called me. I recall the telephone conversation all too well. "Nancy, this is your brother, Jim. I need your help! I am dying of leukemia. I have just left Rex Hospital in Raleigh, North Carolina, and they are telling me that nothing else can be done for me. Nancy, I'm scared!"

I could hardly believe it. To hear Jim's voice was wonderful, but the news—it couldn't be true! Jim was too young to die. He was only sixty three years old; just two years younger than me. "Jim," I said, choking through tears, "come to Florida. I will help you. Give me a few weeks to get the house set up, if you can."

"Okay," Jim said, "I will get train tickets. Will you pick me up at the station in Tampa?"

"Of course," I said. "We will be there."

Jim continued, "Nancy, I will not be a burden to you. I will pay my way."

"Jim, don't even worry about that. I'm not concerned about any of that. You just come on, and let's get you well."

"Okay, Nancy." Jim added, "I'm depending on you, Kid."

I certainly needed a few weeks and then some to get the house in order. My husband, Duane, was still building our very small retirement home. Our home is actually a one-bedroom cottage that is situated beside our son and daughter-in-law's home. My husband was in the process of building our cottage from the skeletal remains of the old horse barn. We lived in three small rooms—a bathroom, small bedroom, and a kitchenette/living room. Duane had barely started building the second phase of the cottage, an open concept room that would house a larger living room, office, and a very tiny dining nook.

Where in the world, I mused, *would we be able to put Jim?* Of course, he would need our bed and bedroom. So where would we sleep? Duane hurriedly framed in the second phase of our home, which was unfurnished boards and flooring. We bought a second-hand queen-sized sofa bed. My husband I were medical missionaries most of our married life, so we were well acquainted with the sciences of "make do" and "manage." We bought a doll-sized dining room table and entertainment center from Goodwill, and we retrieved our dining room chairs from storage. God blessed us, as He always does, and we were able to buy a television and two La-Z-Boy recliner chairs within our very modest budget. Duane and I were satisfied; we would be able to cope with this living arrangement.

My husband and I are naturopathic doctors, or N.D.s. We worked in the missionary field, traveling from coast to coast of this great country helping the needy and the economically and socially disenfranchised. We knew very well that cancer is a disease that cannot be ignored. We had helped many people suffering from this plague, and I myself had been healed from ovarian cancer twelve years prior. We definitely had a problem, and it had to be addressed immediately and aggressively. What were we to do first? We knew that we didn't have that answer yet, but God did. We had to trust Him, for He would provide the answer just as He has always done.

As Duane and I continued down the long corridor to the luggage area of the train station, I heard from behind me, "Hi Nancy." I turned and behind me stood Jim's six foot, three inch frame—sure enough, it was Jim! That broad, impish smile with his twinkling, Irish eyes and graying red hair sticking out of his African doc-tori hat; yes, sure enough, it was Jim. But what happened to the rest of him? He looked like he'd walked out of a concentration camp. His cheeks were sunken in and his face was wrinkled and yellowed. His long arms looked like sticks with hardly any muscle attached. If he hadn't recognized me, I would not have recognized him. He walked slowly and with great pain. It took all his energy to walk to our waiting car in the parking lot.

How Jim had managed on the train by himself for two days, I will never know. But thanks to God, he was here. And as I thanked God for that, I was encouraged that now the miracle of healing would begin.

CHAPTER TWO

Remembering—The Beginning

Jim was born on September 8, 1944, two years and five days after my entrance into the population of planet Earth. World War II was still ragging, so our father, who was on duty aboard a battleship somewhere in the Pacific, missed the blessed event. I wonder to this day if the reason our father never seemed to love or care for Jim was that he missed out on those first years of bonding with his first son.

Except for that first year, Jim and I were always best buddies. I think that the most comfortable and secure place for a baby must be nestled on her or his mother's chest and nursing from the mother's fountain of life-giving love and sustenance. My mother told me years later about how I bit her nipple because she would not allow me to nurse at the same time my baby brother was nursing. Jim was born and I didn't like that interloping bundle of joy very much. That jealousy didn't last very long, though.

While our father was at war, our mother, Jim, and I lived with our maternal grandparents, Clyde and Pauline Davis. I loved my grandparents very much, especially my grandpa. I was never happier than when I sat in his lap playing with his watch, which was tied to his overalls by a shoe lace. I played with the watch while he read the newspaper. I found that when my mother was busy caring for Jim, I could nestle and coo with my grandfather. He told me that I was the best little girl that the good Lord could have sent to his family. In fact, he often told me that I was perfect, but not as perfect, of course, as he was. I was close, though; third after himself and Grandma Minnie. This was a secret we shared. How I loved that wonderful old man!

Those happy days were not to last, unfortunately. Trouble was rearing its ugly head, beginning with Grandma Minnie. She was diagnosed with manic-depression, now known as bipolar disorder. Because of this mental imbalance, she and my mother locked horns often. Grandma often accused my mother of outrageous things, including desiring to have an affair with her own father. Years ago, psychiatric doctors did not understand how hormonal imbalances cause problems like this. Many psychiatric patients, including my grandmother, were treated only with shock therapy and lived grievous and unhappy lives. My grandmother was often away at one sanitarium or another to suffer yet another shock therapy sequence.

As my grandmother's accusations against my mother increased, we moved from my grandparents' home to a little cottage up on the mountain road. Jim and I missed our grandfather desperately.

The war was fast coming to an end. The newspapers and radio caroled the breaking story that Hitler had killed himself and his mistress and that the defeated Axis powers were surrendering to the Allied nations. Our mother was overjoyed; her husband, our father, was coming home.

The war, however, had changed our father. He had seen too much death and destruction. He'd lived on the edge of death for so long that he wanted to live a very exciting and hedonistic existence before he died.

Coupling that with the fact that he was the son of Irish immigrants who ran a bordello and who pimped his sister into prostitution, one can perhaps understand why my father's moral compass was very lacking.

I have often wondered why and how my mother ever saw anything desirable in my father. To be sure, he was handsome and charismatic, but he was also a coarse and uneducated man. My mother was a beautiful blonde, highly intelligent, registered nurse. The fact that they were unequally yoked in social status and education caused many heated and even violent battles between them.

My Grandparents could not understand why my Mother married my Father. I will always believe that it was a re-bound marriage. My Mother met and loved a Jewish doctor while doing her nurses training in Montreal Canada. The doctor's parents did not accept my Mother because she was not a Jew. The doctor loved my Mother and wanted to marry her anyway. But my Mother's pride was hurt and, so she ended their relationship. Soon after that, she met my Father when he delivered bread and pastries to my Grandparents' residence and business.

It didn't take my Father long to convince my Mother to marry him. She was so vulnerable from losing her first love. My Father was Roman Catholic and Mom was English Protestant. James Gordon Carroll and Symola Lucy Davis were married in October, 1941.

I think many people were unhappy with the nuptials that day, especially my Grandparents on both sides of the family. The Roman Catholic priest that officiated the marriage, asked my Father, when my Mother refused to rear her children Catholic, why Father couldn't find a Catholic girl.

My Mother and Father left my maternal Grandparents residence in Belmont, Vermont and moved to Claremont, New Hampshire where my Father's bakery delivery job was located. They settled down in a little apartment on Summer Street. Their first year of marriage was reasonably happy and during that time, I was born, Nancy Lee Carroll, on September 3, 1942. The hospital record states that the charge for my delivery and hospital stay for my Mother and me was $35.00. Imagine that!

After I was born, my Mother had less time to spend with my Father. My Father felt neglected and began cheating on my Mother. At first my Mother didn't believe it and turned a blind eye to the situation. Then my Father was called to war, and he joined the navy and was sent to serve on a battleship in the Pacific. Jim was conceived when my father was home on leave and was born two years later.

Three years later our Father returned home from the war and re-entered civilian life. He hated it; he did not want a wife and two children on his back to support. To him, we children were just accidents happening as a result of his pleasure moments.

The arguing, fighting, including physical violence continued and got progressively worse. Jim and I, still very young, perhaps 5 and 3 respectively, would crouch down behind the bed in the bedroom we shared, and be terrorized that Daddy was going to kill Mommy this time. Jim wouldn't have been more than 6 years old, when Dad started beating him with a leather strap for some supposed infraction that would allow him to take his frustrations out on Jim. I would beg him to leave Jim alone and hit me instead. He never did, and I later learned that he had more deviant plans for me.

When Jim was in the 5th grade, he started stuttering very badly. The more he stuttered in our father's presence, the more Dad would yell at him and punish him. Jim didn't even have peace at school. His teacher Mrs. Davies was a tenant of our father's current mistress, Helen. Mrs. Davies liked Helen, and hated my father for using her as he did. Miss Davies took out her anger on Jim, and made fun of his stuttering in reading class so that the other students would laugh at him. Jim did so badly that school year he had to repeat that grade. Thank God, he was given another teacher the next year. From that setback, Jim got the opinion that he was stupid. The fact was that our father told him he was stupid and worthless so many times he began to believe it. That failure charted his academic progress throughout grade school, junior high, and high school.

When I was 6 years old, and Jim was 4, our younger brother Mike was born. Our Mother tried to stay home and care for us, but our Father gave her so little money for expenses, that she was forced to go back to work as a nurse at the local hospital. My Father bought horses, saddles, and hunting dogs and spent much money on his mistresses, but he demanded that our Mother work to support the family.

One night at about 9:00 PM, mother awakened me from sleep. She had been crying again. "Nancy, she said, "I have taken a job at the hospital. I must start tomorrow. You must take care of your brothers when I am gone. When you are at school, the neighbor, Ann, will look after them, but when you get home, you are in charge again. You've got to feed them, change their clothes, and keep them clean, and safe. I have no one else, Nancy! I'm depending on you! I am giving them to you—to look after". I was 6 years old, Jim was 4 and Mike was a baby. I was in charge of the house, two children and myself.

Once afternoon after the neighbor had gone home and left me in charge, Mike was screaming. He was hungry and wanted his bottle. I couldn't get the nipple to fit over the glass bottle, As I shook to the screams of Mike, I spilled more and more of the milk. Somehow, I don't remember how, Mike got fed that day.

I didn't know how to clean properly, and keep all of us clean. Mike was in diapers and it's funny, but I don't remember changing him; yet I know I did. I wonder if I have blocked some of those details out.

I could not have kept us very clean because all we had to wash in was the sink basin. The old tub had been removed long ago for want of repairs. It was replaced by a rickety old shower that my Mother stuffed full of clothes. Obviously we could not use the shower. I often looked longingly at the shower desiring to take a proper bath.

I prepared meals from food that my mother placed in the refrigerator and the food pantry. I have always been a very visual person so I tried to make the food "pretty". As a six year old surrogate mother, I made my brothers peanut butter and marshmallow and pickle sandwiches. I did add to the menu a glass of milk and a Little Debbie snack. Jim remembered those sandwiches, even as an old sick man, and always loved them.

When all three of us went to school, I, of course, was in charge of getting us up in time to meet the bus. Often time, it was a guess as to whether we would make it or not. Our Mother would pack a school lunch the night before consisting of peanut butter and jelly sandwiches, maybe some chips, and packaged fruit pie. I was always very tired when I got up in the morning, and so there was never enough time or energy to make and eat breakfast, so we didn't. It was hard to stay awake during the morning school hours especially around ten or eleven o'clock. My stomach started to growl and it was very hard to concentrate. I'm sure my brothers didn't fare any better than I did. One morning while sitting at my desk at school, I fainted. After regaining my senses, the teacher sent me down to the lunch room to get a carton of milk and a grapefruit. I wasn't sure what a grapefruit was because I had never seen one. I looked for some sort of grape and obviously could not find it. My brothers and I suffered from what we now know is hypoglycemia. We ate so much sugar because it tasted good, that our blood sugar was always on low pilot.

One winter during a skating outing, my brother Mike broke his leg. My father happened to be home at the time, and I ran to the house to get help. It is hard for me to believe, even to this day, that my father swore and screamed at Mike to stand on his feet and stop horsing around. It is little wonder that the doctor later found cysts in my brother's leg bone. I was feeding my brothers so much junk food because it was already prepared and packaged to eat and "pretty".

My brothers and I slept upstairs in a very ramshackle old farm house. There was very little insulation in the upstairs part of the house. In the winter the temperature outside would drop to minus 10, 15 or even 20 below sometimes. I imagine that it wasn't much warmer in our bedrooms. I the morning the window would be caked with ice from the condensation of our breath. My brothers and I never knew about sheets and pillowcases. We slept on an old filthy mattress and used probably even older chicken down pillows. We did have plenty of blankets, though, but of course they were never cleaned. In fact the house upstairs was never cleaned. My parents slept down stairs in the heated part of the house.

Because of the unsanitary living conditions, Jim, Mike, and I were always getting sick. We got boils and carbuncles, many skin problems, and bleeding noses. Our noses would be coated with scabs and would bleed when we blew them.

As I remember those early childhood years and all the abuse, both physical and mental, that we lived through, I am impressed that if we were youths in a similar environment today, we would be placed in a foster home. Jim especially was severely abused. There seemed to be no safe hiding place for him. Only as he huddled with the old hound dog in the small box house, could he be safe from the wrath of our Father and from the lashes of his whip. A child needs to feel safe and loved at home. We children felt neither of these things.

I felt a deep sense of responsibility to keep my brothers safe and when I couldn't, I felt as if I failed them. No matter how I would plead with our father to stop hurting our mother and the boys, he would not stop.

My father did not beat me, but I found myself, as I developed the body of a young lady, having to defend my honor against my own father. One day as I was washing up in the sink, my Father entered the bathroom. I was completely naked as I was standing at the sink. He started caressing me and telling me that it was alright. He assured me that he was doing nothing wrong and that he had even changed my diapers when I was a baby. I was always a plucky girl and told him to stop or I would tell Mom. When I said that he stopped what he was doing. I praise God that this situation never occurred again and that my perverse father knew that I would tell my mother about his actions that day.

When children live in dysfunction of this nature it sets a pattern for the rest of their lives as to what they perceive as normality. I believe that only with Divine intervention can children brought up in this wickedness live normal life as they grow into adults. Thank God that He will never let go of our hands and will always carry and lift us out of the cesspool of depravity. Thank you, Heavenly Father, and Amen!

CHAPTER THREE

Remembering—The Teen Age Years

During the teen years as Jim and I matured, we started to develop different interests. I always had musical abilities and so I pursued that. It was one of the few times in my young life that I felt any self-worth. It was amazing to me that my parents took little interest in my music, but it did afford them some notoriety when I got chosen to sing solos or when my picture appeared in the local newspapers for something that I had done.

Jim was growing up. I mean, he was really growing! In order to survive, he had to get rough and tough, but in his heart he was a sweet spirit. Our father didn't want a soft son. He wanted a football player son who would bring prestige to the family. Our father wanted to be a football player but wasn't big enough or gifted enough to make the grade. He figured that Jim was big enough and he was going to pound gifted enough into him. He was going to see to it that Jim would make it.

It was about this time that Jim had an experience with God. Jim needed someone to talk with and protect him apart from me. Somehow, when he finally learned how to read, he found a personal relationship with God. Jim was so happy relating with his new Friend that he started carrying a Bible around everywhere with him. When our father found out about this new relationship, he would have none of it; when Jim said that he wanted to be a minister – well, that was not going to happen if our father had anything to do with it. So – Jim got another beating or maybe more, I don't remember.

Jim tried to tell our father that he didn't want to play football, but our father wouldn't listen to him. He didn't care what Jim wanted. This was what he wanted and that was all that mattered. He threw my brother Mike and Jim into the car and drove them down to the football field. Mike told me later that our father had told Jim that if he didn't play hard and beat people up, he would get more beatings. Jim was in tears the whole trip to the football practice.

When they reached football practice, our father presented Jim and Mike to the coach. Mike was still too young to really play, but Jim wasn't. Our father directed the coach to push him hard. Jim was used to being pushed hard, and he was praised by the coach when he played hard. I think my brother would have done anything to receive praise from a father figure. Because Jim was so big, he could intimidate the players with his size. In fact the players called Jim - "BIG JIM" and he really became the work horse of the team.

I can remember Mike telling me about one football practice. The junior varsity squad was not performing to its maximum potential or so the coach thought. He determined to stop the underachieving by using Jim. He paired Jim up with the best performing junior squad player. The coach winked at Jim and said, "Show him how to do it!" The poor junior varsity player didn't have a chance. Jim hit him so hard, he broke the junior varsity player's helmet into. The poor junior also received a concussion. Jim received much more praise for this effort, and he wanted and longed for attention from anyone so much, especially a father figure, that he wanted to hit and hit and hit more players and disable them if he could. I've never liked football because I can't understand anyone wanting to hurt someone else to get their dirty hands on a BALL.

"Big Jim" became the star of the varsity squad. He helped make that team, they were undefeated and the best team in New Hampshire during the 1963 football season. His picture hangs in the Hall of Fame Honor Wall at Steven's High School until this very day. I have a duplicate picture hanging in my home. Brown and Penn State University scouts expressed interest in Jim. They talked about the possibility of a full four year scholarship.

Jim was named All State Offensive and Defensive Tackle. In 1963 he played in the Vermont and New Hampshire All Star game. He played so hard and gave everything he had. After all, his father was demanding that scholarship and he had to deliver.

The game began and within a split second, Jim was hit by a mammoth opposing tackle. He was down and hurt badly. He had a severe back injury and the surgeon told him he would never play football again. He was told that he was lucky that he could walk, and that his hopes of a career and four year scholarship had abruptly ended.

Football was the only thing that Jim knew that he was good at, and now he could never do it again or he would risk total paralysis. He sunk into depression and "who cares about me attitude". This was his senior high school year. Graduation was looming on the horizon, but Jim didn't care. He didn't complete all his classes. He had to attend summer school to attain enough credits to graduate from high school. The star athlete was mailed his diploma approximately six months after his class graduated.

During this time The New England Conservatory of Music had awarded me a small scholarship and I was away at college. Our mother believed in my music abilities, and she sacrificed to send me to that elite school. She paid the tuition that my scholarship did not cover. Our mother really did sacrifice to send me to school, but she never contacted me by phone or mail while I was going to school in Boston, MA. I guess our mother had all she could deal with at home.

While I was away at school, Jim and Mike tried to manage on the home front. Both Jim and Mike hated my opera records and hated even more my singing, but they missed me so much, they would play my records over and over again.

The emotional and physical abuse continued in the home. Dad berated Jim continually about 'flubbing up' his football scholarship. An argument would ensue, and then Dad would start with the abuse. By this time Jim was big enough and strong enough to have beat up Dad, but he never did! Mike begged Jim to beat their father and make the violence stop. Mike was too small to take on his father, but Jim would not assault his Dad. Jim believed it was wrong to hurt his father. On the other hand, Mike vowed to hurt his Dad as soon as he grew strong enough to do it – and the time came when he did. Our father almost died because of the beating Mike gave him.

Jim finally realized that he had to leave home if he was ever going to find a life free of violence. He visited and Air Force recruiting office where he was invited to enlist. The Korean conflict had just started and our government was looking for young recruits. Jim was sent to Lackland Air Force Base in Texas. He got through basic training with flying colors because he was used to being berated, and he was in top physical condition. After basic training he was sent to Korea.

Korea, for Jim, was a place where anything goes. Every vice was available for the young American soldiers. Jim began a drinking barrage when his feet landed on Korean soil and continued until he left Korea two years later. Along with the hard drinking, he started to smoke cigarettes. Women of all ages were readily available. Korean peasants were poor and many married, as well as young teen age girls, gave their bodies for food to get support for their families by prostituting themselves. Sexually transmitted diseases were spread around in great supply. Jim admitted that he frequented this 'well of desire' with an unquenchable thirst.

Jim seemed to have forgotten God, but praise the Lord, God did not forget Jim.

Jim was detailed to an Air Force back up unit run by the United States Army. This unit actually ran an army covert spy operation and was stationed on the DMZ. (Demilitarized Zone) This area was drawn up to separate North and South Korea. It was Jim's job to keep the power plant operational. Jim found himself leaving behind a abyss at home for despotic conditions in Korea. He was stationed in Mae Bong and Seoul, Korea. Part of his duty was to help the ROK *(Republic of Korea)* soldiers. He would spray defoliants like Agent Orange on forested land and transport nuclear and other hazardous waste away from the power plant. Jim never knew that he and other American GI's serving on the DMZ in Korea were deliberately placed in harm's way by the United States Government. Because of this service to his country, years later while he was earning a doctorate degree in divinity, he would be slammed by cancer in the form of CLL. *(Chronic Lymphatic Leukemia)* More will be said about this in a future chapter.

Jim's life and motto while he served in Korea was "party hardy". Remember I said that Jim forgot God, but God did not forget Jim. Thank the Good Lord! When a flood came to Korea, Jim and his platoon were detailed to help in the rescue missions of the Korean people. Jim told me about a gorge and deep river that had over run its banks. Footing was perilous and he was helping to carry heavy equipment through the raging waters. He was the last GI to cross the unstable and precarious bridge. His feet slipped and he tumbled into a whirlpool of torrential water. As he was drowning, a large hand came out of nowhere and scooped him onto dry land and to safety. He never saw the face that the hand belonged to; he just felt this huge force lift him out of the raging water. That day, Jim felt the power of God in a most positive way.

After a two year stay in Hades (known as war time in Korea), Jim returned home to New Hampshire. No home coming could have been so disappointing. As Jim left the taxi, he climbed the stairs to the porch. Our Father greeted him with a "Hi" and then proceeded to get in his car for a liaison with one of his many "ladies of the evening". Jim was in a war zone for two years and Dad couldn't even talk with him for a few minutes. What kind of a father could do this?!

Mom on the other hand was getting ready for work. She was an administrative nurse working the evening shift that night. She screamed and cried all at the same time. The reunion was short lived however, because she was scheduled for duty at the hospital.

Jim found it hard to transition from the party-hardy days of Korea to the life of a civilian. He was bored and he didn't know what direction to go in his life. One of the main reasons that Jim found himself in deep depression was his love for 'Yi Chong'. Yi Chong was a lovely girl that Jim lived with off base in Korea. Some of the American GI's referred to these 'live in's' as *Mooses*. But with Jim it was different – Jim really loved Yi Chong. He knew that his family would never accept Yi Chong as a daughter-in-law and Jim's wife. Our father called all Koreans *'Gookes'*. Jim was living out the great controversy in his heart. It became compounded when Yi Chong got pregnant. Jim wrote a letter 'stateside' to me and told me about his love for her. I assured him that I would love and accept her as my sister-in-law but I readily agreed with Jim that our parents would not accept her. I wish with all my heart that I had not told Jim that, because he paid for an abortion for her and left her in Korea when he returned home. He suffered all his life for that great sin, and he never forgot his love for Yi Chong.

After many months of depression and pining for Yi Chong, Mom and Dad introduced Jim to a young teaching intern called Claire. Claire had just gotten over a broken love relationship and so had Jim. With both on the rebound and hurting over lost loves, Jim and Claire started a relationship that spiraled out of control. Jim was still very much in love with Yi Chong, but married Claire anyway. In my opinion, Jim and Claire should never have married; they were unequally yoked. The Bible has a very serious caution about being unequally yoked. Claire was a Roman Catholic and Jim was a Protestant. Claire would not marry Jim unless he turned Catholic. Jim became a Catholic and was married in the Catholic church. I sang for their wedding. Jim was a Catholic in name only and never practiced the religion in which he didn't believe.

CHAPTER FOUR

Remembering the Middle and Pre-teen Years

When we are young, it seems like the days drag on as one boring day follows another. Now that I am older, I wonder at how fast the days implode upon themselves, and how it seems that another year has come and gone while we are turning around.

I don't think for the most part, we Carroll kids knew what childhood meant. In spite of everything we lived through during our pre-teen years Jim and I were best buddies. Our mother had seen to it that we had bicycles. We often rode together up and down the hills of Winter Street on those bikes. In the spring we enjoyed tramping through our neighbor's field to find pussy willows. Jim and I often had great fun dyeing them different colors. Our neighbors were very good to us. I think they felt sorry for us, and allowed us free access to their property most of the time.

Also in the spring, huge dandelions would grow everywhere in the spring as the meadows transformed from snowy white to verdure green.

Mother and I, not so much Jim and Mike, loved dandelion greens. Our neighbor lady, Ann, was also very fond of this vegetarian delicacy. So Jim and I became dandelion diggers. Through certain times of the year, giant puff ball mushrooms would grow on our hill and Jim and I were the mushroom harvesters. But the best times we had were spent up in the high hills gathering blackberries. We had picking contests to see who could pick the most berries in the shortest time. I always won the contests because I figured out that if I would push the basket high up on my arm, I was free to use both hands for picking the berries, and I didn't eat as many as Jim.

When we were away from the house, Jim was safe. I didn't have to worry that our father would come home in a bad mood and swear at Jim and beat him. Jim and I had moments of being care-free children in the meadow, and we relished every second of it! When we were away from the house, we didn't have to see or hear our mother being beaten and abused.

Mike was more of a loner. He really didn't like tagging after Jim and me very much. He preferred to walk about the woods and explore; when he was old enough, he learned to hunt. Mike learned early in his pre-teen life to eat and sleep at home, but leave as soon as possible. He was beaten as Jim was, and so he found it safer not to be home, even if that meant living at the neighbor's as much as possible, or roving in the woods.

Christmas was an especially sad time. Dad ruined every Christmas that we had at home. Mom dreaded Christmas and said so because of the expense that it brought upon the budget. As children we couldn't understand her concern because she told us that Santa Claus had brought us the presents. Of course we children wanted a Christmas tree. Dad wasn't interested at all in that; like Mom he perceived it an expense that their budget could not afford. When we were older, Jim and Mike and I went off into the deep woods, and after arguing which one was exactly the tree we wanted, would chop it down and drag it home on our sled. We needed our father's assistance to nail a stand on the tree and after much cursing and threats he begrudgingly complied.

My brothers and I wanted to have a fun Christmas like we heard about from our friends at school. We decided to pool the money that we had earned from baby sitting and other odd jobs that the neighbors had hired us for, and buy our parents a present. This year I thought that I had a really good idea. We wanted to give Mom and Dad a very nice gift. I knew that our flat iron was so old and rusty that it was hard to keep from scorching clothes. I knew this very well because it was my job to iron Dad's shirts. I asked my brothers to help me buy a new flat iron for our parents Christmas present. I remember how proud we were to wrap the iron up and put it under the tree. We were beaming when we told Mom and Dad about the lovely Christmas present we had bought them. On Christmas morning we proudly put the gift in our father's lap and of course we told our parents it was for them. My father opened the gift, and threw it against the wall breaking the plastic on the handle. He screamed and yelled at us and said, "How could you have bought such a stupid gift? "No man", he said, "would want such a stupid gift." He then stormed out of the room, got in his car and was gone for the whole day.

Of course we were devastated by this reaction. We had spent all the money we could scrape together and purchased a gift that we thought they needed and would please them. Even though we cried from our father's cruel reaction we knew that for a while Jim and Mike would be safe from persecution and beatings because Dad was gone. We played with the toys Santa had left us – of course provided by our Mother who tried to give us a little Christmas. Our Mother cried and slept most of the rest of the day.

We were always happy and glad when Dad was not home. When he did come home we were always on pins and needles, trying to be good and quiet, because we never knew what would set him off.

Sometimes our mother provoked his wrath. She had caught him cheating yet again. When she confronted him about it, he would curse at her and beat her. He would rip her clothes from her back and beat her with his hands and fist. Often times he would threaten to kill her, but would add he wouldn't do it because he would be sent to jail and she wasn't worth that.

Our Mother wasn't the only one who caught Dad in his indiscretions. I walked into a room often times when our father was in an undressed compromising position with a woman. He would tell me to leave the house, and that I had seen nothing.

To make matters worse, two of the women I saw my father with were our mother's best friends. One of these so called "ladies" conceived a child and had it aborted.

This kind of dysfunction was our world. We saw this and lived it out in our lives day in and day out repeatedly. Male children need the nurture and role modeling of their father to later live successful lives. It is hard for children who live with cruelty to believe even in an all loving Father in Heaven. After all if your earthly father hates and despises you, how could any Father love you? We had no spiritual training at all in our home. The only time we heard God's name mentioned was when His name was used in vain.

We got a glimpse sometimes of what a loving home could be at our maternal grandparents home. Our grandparents loved us very much. They only lived fifty miles away, but we saw them very little. We knew that our grandparents did not fight and abuse each other, but their influence on my brothers was minimal.

We rarely saw our paternal Grandparents, John and Agnes Carroll. They lived in Walpole, New Hampshire. My brothers and I hated going there. The housed reeked of gloom and doom. Our Grandfather, John, died of a massive stroke in his early forties. I saw him only a few times. He was a very muscled man and had a mis-shapened leg. Apparently he had an accident in the Old Country, Ireland. He was a logger, and I am not sure how or why the accident happened. I remember that he looked a lot like my brother Jim including the red hair. Apparently he liked to drink a lot, and squandered what little money he made. He was an abusive husband and absentee father some of the time, so the perpetuation of the "sins of the fathers" continued down the line to our father.

My Grandmother Carroll worked as a chamber maid for hotels and motels. She was uneducated and this was what she could do. In those days with so many Irish people immigrating to America, my grandparents worked at what they could find open to them When they got off the boat they found signs in shops and stores that said, Dogs and Micks (Irish) keep off the grass.

My Grandmother Carroll had seen hard times in Ireland during the potato famine. I never knew or saw a more stern or witchy woman. She was cruel and totally unloving to her children and grandchildren. Mother told me that she pimped her own daughter, Mary, out as a prostitute. My Mother told me that she witnessed the home bordello in operation when she was dating my Father. Mary became pregnant with two illegitimate children as a result of her prostitution. My Mother told me that she tried to abort my cousin Don and this had made him mentally challenged. Mary didn't want or care for these children and left them with Grandmother Carroll to rise. Grandmother Carroll didn't want them either, but she was Irish Catholic and she felt it was her "duty" to rear them. What she really did was put them to work before they were legally able to do so and stripped them of their wages. Ellen, my cousin, was very intelligent and wanted to go to school, but Grandmother Carroll cared little for education; she wanted her to make money.

I remember our Uncle Harold telling about the time when our Father, Gordon, and he came home from school. They were hungry and there was nothing in the ice box. Their Mother, my Grandmother, sat at the table drinking a glass of milk, all the food that was left in the house. She looked at them and said, "I'm sorry boys, but I have to keep up my strength." Then she drank the last of the milk and the boys went to bed hungry.

Our father was a smart man, but he was not allowed to go to school past the third or fourth grade. No indeed, the family needed him to get out and work and help support the home. There was no discussion that he could do both; go to school and work. Absolutely not! There was no money for school clothes or school supplies. Knowing these things, I try to understand my Father, considering all he knew was bitterness, hunger, and disappointments.

I really think our father especially hated his Mother and so his estimation of women was that women were to be used and abused. And I think he really tried to degrade and abuse every woman because of what he perceived that his mother did to him.

The Carroll grandparents' home, to us kids was the original fighting Irish and we were glad that we didn't have to go there often.

In deference to the Carroll grandparents' home, we pined to go to our Davis grandparents' home. Our Mother, Symola Lucy Davis, was the first born of Clyde and Pauline Davis. She was born into a loving but poor and hard working farm family. As stated before, my Grandmother Davis was ill with mental disorder quite often, but our mother experienced a loving family. Mother married my father on the re-bound from a broken romance. When she found herself in a loveless abusive union, she steeled herself to stick it out. It was a family disgrace, in those days, to get a divorce.

Everyone liked my mother and respected her as a nurse. Our grandparents demanded that all of their children finish a college education and our mother became a nurse. She rose quickly in the ranks of her employment and soon found herself in administration. Mother was very successful as a nursing director and later as a hospital administrator. The fact that Mother was an administrator and our father was a maintenance man was also a source of consternation between them. Father felt rather emasculated by Mother's success, and she rather liked the fact that he did.

Even though Mother was a success in her professional life she was totally dysfunctional as a wife, housekeeper, and to a great extent a mother. We lived in a shack; howbeit, there were eleven rooms in the two story fire trap of a house.

Mother was very intelligent; God had given her that gift. But she was always challenged with somewhat poor health. She was a bad asthmatic and had allergies, and like me, I think she suffered from hypoglycemia or low blood sugar. Since she was stressed from her job and her personal life continually she was always tired from the cares of the day. Since she had little energy for anything other than her job, our house never got cleaned. Once in a while the floor got mopped, the trash may have gotten burned and the garbage taken out to the pigs, but that was about it. I really do think our mother tried to cope with housework and cooking, and coping with her children's needs but she didn't have anything left.

I loved our mother and pitied her existence, but the thing that I will never understand is how our mother could see and know that her children were being abused and neglected by her husband and not stop it. This is still beyond my comprehension. Our mother made fairly good money as a nurse. She could have moved us out of that house and supported a new residence. Our mother told us she loved us, but she did not protect us.

When there is physical and emotional abuse in the home, children learn to act and react with it. When a young boy sees his father abuse his mother, he learns to do the same. He will not learn to cherish and respect his mother or any other woman. Both Jim and Mike learned to cope with stress and disappointment with brute force and physical violence. It almost destroyed both of them.

With this mode of living impressed so forcefully in their psyche, they were walking time bombs, as adults they were blueprinted for personal and professional tragedy.

CHAPTER FIVE

Remembering the Young Married Years

As I stated in the previous chapter, Jim and Claire were married in a Roman Catholic Church ceremony. The church looked so beautiful that day and Jim and Claire were so hopeful and looking forward to a happy and productive life. I sang two songs during the ceremony. How I got through the musical selections only God knows. I had severe problems of my own.

I was not well. I was a young married mother with two young boys. My marriage was in trouble and my health was failing. I lived in Wisconsin with my husband, Francis, and two young sons. When Jim asked me to sing at his wedding; I could not refuse. Even though I was sick and could little afford the plane trip, I packed myself and my children and flew to New Hampshire. My husband did not accompany me because he had to work. I developed blood clots in my left leg from the long plane trip and subsequent car ride from Logan Air Port in Boston, Massachusetts to Claremont, New Hampshire. After I sang for the wedding, my leg swelled to three times its normal size. I was in serious pain, even agony. My father was forced to carry me in his arms to the car and rush me to the hospital. I was thankful that Dad did that, but I had to endure his swearing about the inconvenience to himself. I was in the hospital for approximately three days. My oxygen levels dropped so low that I was placed in an oxygen tent. They called my condition tachycardia with accompanying blood clots. I was very worried about my boys and how they would be looked after, but my little sister, Patty, watched after them while my Mother was working.

For Patty, I think my situation was payback time. Patty was born in my Mother's 41st year. Mom and Dad's marriage was never good, and it was getting worse and worse. It is hard to call a child's birth an accident, but Patty was not a child that was planned. I was thrilled when she was born, because I always wanted a sister to love. My Mother even blamed me for her pregnancy because I teased her so often for a sister. Jim was also thrilled when Patty was born. I was almost 17 years old and Jim was 15 when she was born. Jim and I argued over which one could hold, feed, change, and bathe her. Because of this attention, Patty was a very spoiled baby. When Jim and I got off the school bus, Patty would hear the engine, and she would start howling. Jim and I would run into her bedroom, she'd be standing up in her crib with her hands outstretched to be picked up. Because she cried constantly to be kissed and held, we called her "Ruined" and "Missy" for Miserable. These were really loved names that we gave her. Jim changed and cared for her as much as I did. When he started playing football, he even looked after her as she watched him on the sidelines of the practice field.

When Patty was two years old, she developed pneumonia. Since my Mother was a nurse, she tried to care for her at home. Her condition worsened, and Patty was taken to the hospital and placed in an oxygen tent. Mom was working at the hospital as a nurse to pay bills and take care of us. Dad was nowhere to be found. It seemed that he never cared that Patty was very ill and there was a question as to whether she would pull through or not. Mom could not afford special nurses around the clock for Patty, so I was pulled out of school to sit and watch my sister while she struggled in the hospital to hold on to life. Even though she was very sick, she wasn't too sick to be "spoiled". She would stick her little foot out of the oxygen tent to be kissed and rubbed and then she would sleep knowing that her big sister, Nancy, was there watching over her.

I have digressed a little talking about the love that Jim, Mike, and I had for our baby sister, Patty, and now I will continue my narrative about Jim and Claire.

After the wedding, Jim and Claire prepared to leave on their honeymoon. I forgot where they went, but Jim, Claire, my two boys and I found ourselves on the same plane leaving for Madison, Wisconsin. I had just left the hospital and I was on strong blood thinners to dissolve the blood clots, so I could not walk. Jim carried me aboard the plane and I prayed that I would not scare my little sons or die until I got home. Francis met us at the airport and took me immediately to the hospital. When I got into surgery, the doctors could not find a femoral pulse, and I almost lost my leg that day. My leg has been misshaped from that day because of the ballooning effect from the clots.

For the newlyweds, the days merged into months and the settling in process of a merged new life together. Claire was a young special education teacher and Jim was working wherever he could. They decided that Jim needed to receive more education if he was to get a good job. So Jim began studies at the University of Maine on Presque Isle. Claire worked hard to help Jim succeed and to pay the bills. Jim struggled to pass his classes. He received a Bachelor of Arts degree in Education but unfortunately Jim never really liked teaching. He got into trouble with his superiors frequently for incomplete lessons plans, unorthodox teaching practices, and the lack of discipline. God had called Jim to be a Pastor, but Jim had not yet realized it.

Jim and Claire were married about a year when a little son was born. I remember their son; Jimmy was a very loving child and wanted to please everyone. Another son, Peter, was born about a year later but was a very slightly built youngster with a ruddy complexion. Peter was very suspicious, and it took time for him to feel comfortable with strangers. Even though Peter did not trust easily, he loved my son, William. I remember as we left Maine to return home to Wisconsin, Peter cut a little corner from his beloved blanket and gave it to William. William was about 8 years old but was very touched by this loving gesture.

Francis, the boys, and I made a couple more trips to see Jim and family over the next few years. One trip was to Presque Isle and the other was to their new home in Ellsworth, Maine. This was where Jim and Claire had acquired teaching positions, after Jim graduated.

Sarah, the third child was born after Jim began his internship as a new instructor. He seemed so happy to have a little daughter at last, but shortly became restless. He loathed teaching and his marriage to Claire seemed to be unraveling.

Jim and Claire decided to move back to their hometown in Claremont, New Hampshire. Jim began teaching at St. Mary's Catholic school. However, Jim disliked the rules of study and conduct set forth by the Sisters and Principal of the school. He was always at variance with them. Both he and Claire enjoyed being home again, but Jim became unfulfilled and quit teaching.

Jim took a job at the Claremont Daily Eagle newspaper as a cub reporter and distribution manager. He was never very well organized and this job proved to be a nightmare for him. He either quit or was fired again and again from various jobs during the next few years.

Jim finally found a job with the New Hampshire Army Reserves as a recruiter. He loved that job, was happy, and became a very successful recruiter.

About this time, Jim's marriage was disintegrating and he started cheating on Claire. Unfortunately most of the women he dated were women he met while recruiting. Jim's superiors warned him about this philandering but he ignored their warnings. Sadly Jim was fired once again and left the only job that he had really enjoyed.

Claire, by this time had a belly full of Jim's cheating, and neglect. She sued for divorce after 18 years of an unhappy marriage.

Jim decided to move to Plymouth, New Hampshire for a new start. Unfortunately the change of scenery did not change Jim. Jim was depressed and his undiagnosed Bi-polar disease kept him in turmoil. At times he would be flying high and the next day he was extremely depressed. Since Jim was a handsome six foot tall hunk, it was not hard for him to find a woman to shack up with. When a man wants to find an unprincipled, immoral, floozy type woman in this sin sick world they seem to be readily available. Most of the women that Jim shacked up with completely supported him. He would stay with one woman for a time, get tired of her, and then move on to a different liaison.

About this time, Jim's divorce from Claire was finalized. As Jim related in the Preface Chapter, he was 43 and in two weeks' time, he lost his car, his job, income, home, wife, and family. In one giant brush stroke, he seemingly lost everything. In his anguish and despair he came face to face with God in the little chapel, in Plymouth, New Hampshire.

When the little old man beckoned Jim to enter the Chapel, Jim states that this loving stranger read his complete life's story back to him,- read his mail! It was there that Jim accepted God as he repeated the 'sinners' prayer.

Dear reader, I wish with all my heart that I could say that 'once saved –always saved' is really the road to salvation. But that is really not true! Jim did not continue in a saved condition, in fact he back slid into a deeper pit than he found himself before the original conversion experience. Like the character David, of the Old Testament, Jim slid down the slide to perdition and found himself lost and lonely again.

CHAPTER SIX

Remembering the Second Marriage and Half-way House

(Note: Some names have been changed to protect the innocent)

As I stated in the previous chapter, Jim was out of work again. Jim returned to Claremont to live with our Mother. His Bipolar disease was still undiagnosed and it was crippling him. One moment he would be laughing and loud and raucous, and just as quickly, switch and be depressed to the point of suicide. Then one day as he went out for a walk – the unexpected happened.

Her name was Mary Lee. She was tall, statuesque, and blonde. Jim always preferred blonde ladies, I think, because his Mother had blondish hair. Mary Lee was on the rebound, recently divorced from an affluent but emotionally abusive husband. Jim was tall, handsome, and free. Sparks flew and they became an item.

Jim and Mary Lee's relationship was based on dysfunction and co-dependency. Mary Lee was very much a lady and someone Jim could respect. Most of Jim's romantic relationships at that time were one night stands or merely a 'friend with benefits' arrangements. Mary was *different* and the family liked her.

Mary Lee was accustomed to living in a beautiful home and having a liberal allowance to spend. When Mary Lee divorced her husband, she lost the family home and her liberal allowance. Her settlement allowed her to buy a very modest mobile home but she had to get a job to maintain it. She had no marketable skills, and so she worked as a waitress at a local restaurant.

Jim, on the other hand, was as poor as a church mouse. He had no income, no home, no job, and didn't really have enough ambition or self-esteem to get up in the morning to find a job. So Mary Lee worked hard as a waitress, and Jim sometimes worked.

As their friendship developed into a love relationship, they determined that they needed more stability in their lives. So, Jim and Mary Lee started going to church. It wasn't long before they married and for a time they were ecstatically happy.

Jim loved his church and spiritual life and even became a lay pastor. One of his greatest joys at that time was having the opportunity to preach with Mary Lee sitting in the pew lovingly looking up at him. But even among the rose filled moments of his spiritual life there surfaced from out of the blue, the barbed thorns and the dark depression of Bipolar disease. Mary Lee, the family, and I am sure, especially Jim, could not understand this "Jekyll and Hyde" behavior. Also about this time, Jim experiences the first symptoms of Leukemia. He made a doctor's appointment to find out what was going on with his health. The doctor diagnosed him from tests that were done as being in the very early stage of Chronic Lymphatic Leukemia (CLL).

As per Jim's 'modus operandi' he ignored the doctor's diagnoses and the doctor request for more tests and more medical help. He told no one about the medical opinion; even Mary did not know until years later when he was suffering with the last stages of this dreadful disease.

Mary Lee suspected that more than emotional traumas were causing Jim some grief, but she never suspected the full cup of the dysfunctional behavior. She finally went to our Mother with her suspicion but nothing was said to Jim because they knew that Jim would blow off their concerns.

Since Jim and Mary lived in Newport, New Hampshire, the family in Claremont did not see them more frequently than once a month. It was becoming more apparent to my sister and mother that Jim was displaying more and more erratic behavior. Jim couldn't seem to hang on to any job, the primary reason was that he resented any superior or boss telling him what to do. He finally refused to get up and go to work, and so he lost one job after another. All he wanted to do with his time was stay at home, sleep, and watch television.

It was becoming more and more difficult for Mary Lee to work, pay the bills, keep the house work up, and keep up with Jim's increasing sexual appetite. His desire for multiple sexual activities every day was alarming her and wearing her out. Even his conversation was clouded with perverse speech and demands were shouted at her for unconventional sexual activities. Mary finally understood where some of this perverseness was coming from, when she found him watching pornography. Apparently his television viewing was primarily the pornographic television channels. Today, doctors know much more about the symptoms and malaise of Bi-polar disease. Research has shown that perverse sexual speech is part of the symptoms of this disease. How sad it is for me to know that Jim went undiagnosed and without help for years with this unnatural degrading perversion.

As I stated before, Mary Lee, worked to pay all the bills. Their small savings were soon dried up. Jim basically refused to work, and when he did, he couldn't hold on to the job. He defied his bosses and resented all authority. He was fired from one job after another. Even though Mary Lee loved Jim and the Carroll family loved her, she couldn't cope anymore. She had enough of carrying the whole financial and emotional load of the family. Mary Lee soon asked Jim to leave their home. They were both devastated, and Jim found himself alone again! Mary Lee wanted to get on with her life and so she divorced Jim.

Trying to pick himself up from the second divorce was almost a super human thing for Jim to do. He finally reasoned that He needed a new start, and so he sold or gave away everything that he owned. He was determined to leave New Hampshire forever. But then our Mother became gravely ill.

It was about this time that my sister, Patty, called with the unexpected news that our mother was dying. Our mother had a third and fourth stroke. I was called to come home immediately. My sister related to me that our mother had lost her speech, left hand movement, and they believed, cognitive reasoning.

Jim was Mom's favorite child, and I believe that he loved her more than anyone else in the world. It seems most strange to remember how Mom loved Jim and yet she did not protect him as a child from our father's wrath. It took our mother three and a half weeks to die. All four of us kids took turns sitting at her bedside round the clock in the hospital. It was pure agony to watch her urine bag turn darker and darker and watch her life functions slowly ebb away. Jim was sitting at her bed side when she died. Jim, of all four of us, grieved the hardest for our Mother. Jim wanted to get away from all the dark memories and dysfunction of the Carroll family.

Jim and I were still best of buddies, but he even left New Hampshire without saying good-bye to me and telling me where he was going. I suppose it was possible that he didn't know where he was going; he just knew he was leaving.

I was extremely concerned for my brother. I knew he was not healthy and I was constantly polling family members for new information as to where Jim could be. Finally one day my sister, Patty, told me about a Pastor Willy that Jim had met at the Pentecostal Church. She heard that Jim returned to North Carolina with the Pastor where he and his wife ran a half-way house for transients and addicts.

About four years passed. I had been asking family and friends for information about Jim. No one seemed to know anything. Finally I told my brother Mike and sister Patty that I was going to search for Jim. Mike was bitter about Jim ditching the family and told me to 'butt out' and leave Jim alone. He told me, 'that if Jim didn't care about us, then he didn't care about him either.

Patty also had some issues with Jim. Jim had abused Patty's hospitality. In between Jim's marriage and divorce, Jim had stayed with her in her house. Patty stated that he had run up bills that she could not afford to pay. Jim's attitude about this seemingly free loading was that Patty had inherited everything from our Mother's estate, and so he deserved to have compensation for sacrificing his part of the Carroll inheritance. And so, Patty asked Jim to leave our mother's home which she now owned. Our mother had asked us before she died to bequeath our part of the estate to Patty because she was the youngest sibling and was alone and unmarried. Jim did not leave Patty on friendly terms, and there was a lot of strife between them. Patty was not that anxious to ever see Jim again.

Even though I was not encouraged by Mike and Patty to locate Jim, I continued my search. I found a 'locator' who found Jim at Pastor Willy's facility in Raleigh, North Carolina. I was able to talk with Pastor Willy by phone. We had a lengthy discussion. It became apparent that

Jim and he had held many therapy sessions for he knew much about the Carroll personal history. Pastor Willy gave me an overview and up to date scenario of what was happening with Jim. At the end of our discussion, I wasn't that impressed with Jim's progress. I asked Pastor Willy to prevail upon Jim to call me by phone. Pastor Willy thought this to be a good idea and promised he would request this of Jim.

Within the week, Jim phoned me. I was so happy to hear his voice. Jim, however, was not happy to hear my voice and told me so. He basically told me, "Nancy, you've got your life, and I've got mine, don't call me again." And he hung up on me. I was devastated and cried for hours. I had lost my childhood buddy, my dear brother, the one that I shared loneliness and terror with, the brother that I had lost and just found. Now he never wanted to hear from me or see me again.

Even though Jim only spoke a few words to me, I knew he was not happy. My heart strings were torn for days. My constant thought was how I could help my brother.

After a few days of praying for God's counsel to help my brother, I again called Pastor Willy. I relayed to him what had happened when I spoke to Jim. He basically already knew how our conversation had ended because Jim told him that he would not see me or talk to me. Jim had told Pastor Willy that he never wanted anything to do with the Carroll Family ever again. In that conversation with Pastor Willy, I learned that Jim had lost a finger from a farm accident with their resident bull. He had not performed his farm duties with safe practices, and as a result had a finger ripped off. He often times would not show up for work projects; he was also insubordinate with superiors, and had difficulty interacting with many of the other residents. Jim's typical MO had returned to rear its ugly head. Pastor Willy went on to say that Jim had been with them two years, much longer that was expected and even allowed, and just that very day, had told Jim that by the next week he had to leave. The Pastor told Jim that it was time to find and retain a job and get on with his life.

Jim found himself alone and feeling rejected again. He had no more direction on how to get on with his life than as he did when he first started living in the half-way house two years earlier. Again he returned to his lost and lonely condition without hope and despondent.

*From Left to Right: Jim Carroll, age 8;
Mike Carroll, age 3; Nancy Carroll, age 10*

Jim's football picture. The undefeated football team picture still stands in the Hall of Fame, Steven's High School, Claremont, NH

Combat in Korea

Jim Carroll and friends, stationed on the DMZ Spy Station, Korea

*Jim Carroll, age 22,
soon after graduating form high school*

*Jim Carroll, (late 30s or early 40s)
during his teaching years*

Jim Carroll and Dr. Terri McEndree, shortly before Jim's death.

Picture just before Jim's death with Sister Nancy

From Left to Right: Duane McEndree, Jim, and Charles McEndree

CHAPTER SEVEN

Remembering Leaving The Half Way House And Living on the Street

As Jim closed his suitcase with all his worldly possessions in it, he gave one more painful virulent look at his room as he turned off the light. This had been his home for the last two years. He was in his late forties now, and these few possessions were all he had to show for his life.

Pastor Willy and his wife had finally demanded that Jim get on with his life and leave the halfway house. The Pastor and his wife had been very good to Jim, Jim told me later how he defied their instructions and advice. He continually violated house rules and was often insubordinate to his counselors. A typical rehab stay at the halfway house was approximately 6 months, and Jim had been there two years. The Pastor told me when we spoke by phone, that he had seen little progress in Jim in those two years. Jim seemed to be content in doing as little as possible and defying all authority as much as possible. From the Pastor's perspective, the situation with Jim became insufferable and outrageous, and for the good of all the other clients, teachers, and counselors, it was time for Jim to move on.

Jim was dropped off in the city of Jonesboro at a prearranged location holding his suitcase, his only possession. In his suitcase was a change of clothes, his hat, a few personal things, and his Bible. He didn't know where he was going or even how to get anywhere, and he had very little money.

My brother lived a rough life, but he never lived on the street before. How he was going to live, he did not know. Jim had served in Korea and learned how to live the spartan life of a soldier, but there at least he was backed up by his army buddies. Now he found himself in a strange city, on the street, and without a friend. Jim was a big tall man, approximately 6'3" and 250 pounds, and he knew how to use his brawn, so maybe this impressed or intimated the street dwellers. Whatever the case, the brawn or the brain, the street residents accepted Jim quite readily and treated him as one of their own. There he had lived with the street veterans, the drunks, the pimps, the prostitutes, and the transients, who are mostly an invisible presence on the streets and under bridges in most large cities. These 'low-life's' that God loves and sent his Son to die on the cruel cross for are considered at best an eye sore and a nuisance to most decent society. On these cruel and decadent streets live a multi-cultural clan, but the vast majority of the people, are black Americans. Jim's street friends gave him a new street name. They called him "White Chocolate".

I believe that Jim, at first until his money ran out, slept in flop houses and mission beds, but soon even that would sometimes be unavailable. After his money ran out, his street friends showed him how to get by, feed and clothe himself. There were soup kitchens for daily sustenance and good will stores for clothes. There were clinics for oral health needs, pillows and blankets for warmth and even good books to read. He would wash up in the bathroom of a Hardees or McDonald's restaurant, and if he was fortunate, he might find a hospital or other restaurant with a bigger bathroom where he could clean up. Sometimes he could wash his clothes in a laundry washing machine or dryer that was unattended. Restaurants, new businesses, or open houses, often had free food available, and if you knew what dumpsters to look into, on a good day, perfectly good food that was not sold, was available. The street people even showed Jim where to find discarded clothes. Of course there were also the street missions that provided beds and meals and clothes for the down and outers of society of which Jim was one.

Jim lived like this for many months, eating, drinking, and sleeping wherever he could find a big enough hole to climb into. On occasion, he would find a temporary job, but that wouldn't last long. Ironically Jim found comrades and friendship on the streets. Even though, this time seemed to be the lowest ebb in Jim's life, he had a demeanor of peace and happiness. Jim had descended in social status from a school teacher and honored professional, to a down and out street bum. Howbeit, even then, a quiet peace enshrouded his frame. At last he had found acceptance and compassion from a motley group of friends who seemed to understand his plight.

Life on the streets for Jim was very monotonous at times; he went to bed when he felt like it and got up when he felt like it. The mission beds had rules for lights out and getting up time. Also, Jim never knew when a street fight would break out or a drug deal would go bad. The streets certainly had their share of action. There were street rules too! Everybody minded their own business and ratting out to the police was not accepted or tolerated. Such was the life on the street for Jim.

For whatever reason, Jim did not spend a great deal of time relating to me about his life on the streets of Jonesboro. I don't really know why I didn't get more information about this time of his life. I think he just wanted me to know that he had a rough time on the streets, yet in a very strange way, it was also a happy and contented time for him.

After many months of living on the streets, Jim decided to better himself and take a federal test and apply for a federal job. The day Jim took the test was a good day for him; he passed the test with flying colors. Because he was a Korean Veteran, he was awarded even more points for a higher score. Jim was given a postal job at the United States Post Office in Jonesboro, North Carolina. He loved this job. He was earning good money and even had a nice place to live, but then it happened! When Jim was placed in the postal job, he told them that he was going to be attending college at night school to finish his master's degree. His superiors agreed that Jim's working schedule would not change, and he would not have to work the night shift. Unfortunately, as I learned from my own experience working for the United States Government, government bosses often tell employees what they want them to hear, and they do not always tell the truth of keep their promises. In the middle of a work week, Jim's schedule was shifted to the night shift. This, of course, meant that Jim could not attend night classes to finish his master's degree. Getting a divinity degree was Jim's dream; his lifelong dream was to be a pastor. Jim very sadly quit his postal job when he could not get his boss to keep his word and not annex him to the night shift. I have found from my own experience that often government supervisors are less than honest and many are ruled by politics, cronyism, and nepotism. In my opinion there is little honesty and integrity in the promotional system of the U. S. Government as I found out first hand by working for the VA and dealing with them for medical help at a later time for Jim. I will elaborate on this in another chapter.

Jim was down and out financially again, but his dream had come alive in his heart. He didn't know how he was going to do it, but with God's help, he was finally going to be a Pentecostal Pastor!

CHAPTER EIGHT

Remembering Pastor Helen And Shaw University

After Jim quit the postal job, he was as it were, on the skids and streets again. He had no money and no way to pay for a house or even a room, food or clothing. He didn't know how he would get by; but no matter, he knew somehow he was going back to school. He knew God was calling him into His service to become a pastor of the Gospel of Christ. It was about this time that he met Pastor Helen and her associates.

Pastor Helen was an evangelist who brought the Word of God to the street people. Her pulpit was the street and her congregation was the outcasts on the street. She was also a divinity professor at Shaw University in Raleigh, North Carolina. I believe that she also pastored a church that the transients and people like Jim frequented from time to time. Whatever the case, Pastor Helen and her associates met Jim during an evangelistic service. She reached out to Jim, and Jim responded to her Christ-like commission. Pastor Helen and her colleagues helped Jim find work and a way that he could become a student at Shaw University.

I know that Jim was never a good student in academics, and I am sure that Pastor Helen and the other professors tutored Jim and helped him complete his master's program. Jim was blessed abundantly at Shaw. He was one of three or four white students to graduate at that time from Shaw University. They called him by his street name, "White Chocolate". He was their brother in Christ Jesus, and they loved him and Jim loved them as well.

This was a time in Jim's life that I did not share and I must rely on information that he shared with me. As I write this narrative realize I must remember that it is now going on five years since Jim's death. It has taken me this long to put some of my thoughts to paper because some of these images cause me much pain and sorrow to remember. I almost re-live them again, and they also make me miss my brother so very much. Even so I must fulfill my promise to Jim and finish this book.

Even though I did not share in Jim's life at this time, I did have the opportunity on two occasions after Jim's death to talk to Pastor Helen. Actually, I think I talked with her once before Jim died. Never the less, Pastor Helen was good enough to send me Jim's diploma, cap and gown.

After Jim graduated with a Master's degree in divinity from Shaw University he was soon accepted to begin a doctoral program from that same university. Jim was planning on finishing his Ph.D. in two years and then going to South Africa with other colleagues to start Christian elementary and secondary schools. While Jim was working on his doctorate, he was also working as a chaplain at Rex Hospital in Raleigh, North Carolina.

Jim talked to me many times about the miraculous healings at that hospital that he had personally witnessed. He even related to me on one occasion of seeing a person growing a perfect arm from a withered limb. Praise the Lord! It must have been more than thrilling to see this wonderful miracle of God. But Jim also told me about one particular case that tried his personal relationship with God.

Her name was Susan. She was a young wife and mother. Jim told me that she was only thirty-one years old. She was admitted to Rex Hospital suffering from the last stages of Ovarian Cancer. Jim was her case worker and of course he met her husband and young two year old daughter. This was an emotionally wrenching case, and Jim let his heart become very attached to these dear people. Jim never could learn to detach himself from his client's personal problems. As Jim watched the family suffer through Susan's chemotherapies, radiation, and surgeries, he began reassuring the husband and father that he was sure that Susan would be healed. He told the husband that he had prayed and that he believed that God had told him that Susan would be spared and healed. When Susan subsequently suddenly died, Jim was devastated. "How could this be; he wondered, "How could I have been so wrong!" "How could God have done such a thing?" "Why did God leave this very young child motherless?" Jim's faith was rocked to its very core. Jim told me he told God not to even talk to him. Jim asked for an immediate leave of absence from the hospital, took to his bed, and basically dropped out of life for a while. After that very long week, Jim received this letter that I found pasted in his journal.

Dear Jim,

My thoughts and prayers are with you almost every day. Your Christian love for Susan and our family was God sent, and I praise Jesus for being with you. I went through angry thoughts and hopelessness. Life on Earth is our responsibility; it is up to us to accept God's answers to our prayers. We must let go of that which is not of God and go forward to make our lives useful. You helped to give

Susan and our family peace. I miss Susie. She was special, and my love for Susie is with me always. The tears came a great deal. I carry her beneath my heart, and there she will always be.

God bless you, Jim, and keep praising the Lord in song.

Bob and Dot (daughter) Ford

One of God's servants once told me that the world will estimate your importance by the number of people serving you, but God is more concerned with the number of people you are serving. A spiritual marker identifies a time of decision when each one of us clearly knows that God is guiding us. Although He will clearly guide us there are very few people God can trust (consider the prophets) that they will speak for Him. God's kingdom completely rejects worldly honor and the world's measure for esteem. God cannot trust most people to claim His authority. He conversely gives the greatest honor to those who serve in the lowly realm of humility and in divine trust and obedience to God.

I believe Jim understood that never again could He claim to know God's mind; rather it was his lot to embrace and accept God's will.

CHAPTER NINE

Remembering Ruby and A Life Changing Event

As Jim was making his early morning rounds on that fateful day, he knew that he really did not feel very well. He had not really felt very well for some time. He shared his concerns with his good friend Ruby, but no one else. He also demanded that she tell no one about his concerns. As he left his office to begin seeing his first patient, he fainted in the corridor. Someone soon found him on the floor and helped him to his feet. He made some lame excuse about low blood sugar, and assured his rescuer that he would eat something and then begin his rounds.

He staggered to the cafeteria and drank a large glass of orange juice. After sitting in the cafeteria booth for about fifteen minutes, he seemed to feel a little better. "Well, I'm all right now," Jim thought, "I've got to start my rounds.", "Off you go!" he said to himself. After walking only a few steps, Jim fainted again. This time orderlies came to help and Jim awoke to find himself on a bed in the emergency room. A barrage of tests was ordered by the doctor. Of course it took some time for the tests to be completed and read by the physicians, but then the test results were there and read to Jim. It wasn't good. All tests were positive. When the doctors questioned Jim about his symptomology, Jim related that he often broke out in full body sweats, had enlarged lymph nodes, especially in his neck and groin, often times had migraine like headaches, a very much enlarged abdomen with much pressure, and many other symptoms. When the doctors questioned Jim as to why he had told no one about these health problems, his answer was he had prayed that they would go away. Unfortunately these problems had persisted for more than ten years. This unfortunately was typical of Jim. If Jim didn't want to face some unpleasantness, he would simply run away from it. This time, his typical response would not work. He positively could not run from this situation.

As the week progressed, Jim fainted many times. In one day, he fainted four times. For his personal safety and that of others, he was suspended from his work at the hospital. Then a few days later, Jim was asked to come to the hospital for a consult with his primary physician. Jim was told that he was in the fourth and final stage of chronic lymphatic leukemia, a morbid disease characterized by excessive leucocytes or white blood cells in the blood. And the doctors, who knew and worked with Jim, also informed him that even if he resigned himself to chemotherapy, he probably would not live for more than six months.

Jim agreed to chemotherapy and radiation as a lifesaving therapy. Only Pastor Helen and Ruby were there for Jim as he suffered the painful and exhaustive rounds of nausea that accompany chemotherapy. When these therapies did not give enough relief, they did surgery to drain fluid off his lung. By now Jim's spleen had grown to a mammoth size; the surgeon had recommended a spleenectomy. His spleen was so large that Jim looked pregnant, and it was displacing all of his internal organs. The doctors also advised Jim that he probably would not live through the surgery. They said he would probably bleed to death because the spleen was full of blood. Jim prayed about having the surgery and decided not to have it.

Ruby was always there for Jim. She finally demanded, and would not take no for an answer, how to contact Jim's family. Ruby was terribly concerned because the prognosis for Jim was very grave. Jim was growing weaker and thinner every day. Jim returned home to his small efficiency apartment in the ghetto and basically slept almost around the clock. Ruby checked on Jim every day, and was unrelenting to know who in the family Jim wanted to notify about his health. One day Jim did not answer the door when Ruby came by to see him. Ruby had the superintendent of the building break down the door to see about Jim. They found him very weak and barely conscious and had him rushed to the hospital once again. He was in and out of the hospital for weeks at a time. This was a continuing saga for Jim. Finally with much persuasion on Ruby's part, Jim promised to call me. One night, very late at night, the call came.

CHAPTER TEN

Remembering Jim's Phone Call

I had quite resigned myself to believe that I had lost my brother and would never hear from him again. Jim had made that perfectly clear when he was at the half way house. He even demanded that Pastor Wiley reinforce his declaration that he never wanted to hear from me again or any of the other Carroll family members. He ended his conversation to me before he abruptly hung up by saying, "You have your life and I have mine, Goodbye!" Since that very sad day, I really learned not to think of Jim very much anymore.

I believe it was September, 2007, very late at night when the phone rang. It was about 11:00 p.m. I remember thinking "Who in the world could be calling us this late at night? I stumbled out of bed and through the sleep haze I answered with a very weak, "Hello". "Hello, Nancy this is your brother, Jim," came the response. Could this be, I thought through my sleep haze. Yet, no one had to identify that voice. It was Jim after all these years; it was the voice of my brother. "Nancy", Jim said, "I'm sorry for calling you so late at night, but I'm scarred and I need your help." "What's the matter, Jim?" I questioned. "I'm dying, Nancy, the doctors have told me that they have done all they can. I'm scared and I need to talk to you. I know it's late, but I'm scared". I could barely breathe. I was finally talking to my beloved brother who I had lost, and now that I had found him, I was going to lose him again.

"Jim", I said, "Come to Florida and Duane and I will help you." I then asked Jim to briefly tell me about his physical disease and medical prognosis. When he concluded relaying to me about the cancer and the therapies that he had endured, I reiterated that he should come to Florida and my husband and I would help him. Jim knew that Duane and I are naturopathic doctors. We have helped many people be healed by following God's methods of healing cancer and other diseases. I, myself, had been diagnosed as having ovarian tumors with a doctor's prognosis about twenty years earlier. Jim answered that he would like to try God's healing methods. I asked him how long it would take him to come to Zephyrhills. He told me that he believed he needed at least two weeks to pack, buy the train ticket, and close up his apartment. I tried to get him to come more swiftly, and to fly, but he insisted on coming by train. Jim was crying intermittently throughout the conversation. I asked that we have prayer and that we believe that God can do anything including healing him of cancer. As our conversation concluded, I hung the phone up. I was weeping as softly as I could so as not to awaken Duane. He would need to be told about this problem as soon as he awoke. I had a little guilt twinge as I remembered that I had not even asked Duane about the arrangement with Jim. I just blurted out my decision for Jim to come as soon as he could get here. Even though I should have discussed the arrangement with Duane, I knew my husband would readily agree that we must do whatever it took to get Jim well.

As I sat in my lounge chair softly weeping, I started feeling so sorry for myself and especially sorry at how unfair life was for Jim. Jim was still so young; only sixty-three years old. He saw and lived through so much sadness and tragedy, and as far as I was concerned, lived without joy, love, and happiness. How could a good God allow this to happen, I wanted to know. Pictures of violent abuse from the past from when we were children flooded my mind. It wasn't Jim's fault that he was born into such a sick, hateful, and dysfunctional family. "Where was the fairness in that?", I asked God. I could feel my blood pressure rising and the pain in my neck and eyes as the pressure pummeled inside the arteries. I just kept repeating, "how could this be, how could this be." And then I shifted my focus. "O my Lord", I said to God. "Where will we put Jim?" As I stated in the beginning of this book, Duane was building our little retirement cottage from the skeleton remains of a horse barn. We had basically three little rooms to live in, a bedroom, bathroom, and a kitchen with a little nook for 2 chairs and a little miniature TV set. Plans were being made as soon as we had enough money, to add on a combination living room, and dining room. Jim was going to be with us in two weeks! Where were we all going to sleep?! I had no idea. In this confused state I picked up a pencil and paper and started to write this poem.

<u>Overcoming In Christ</u>

How did you tackle your burdens today?
With a resolute heart and a confident way?
Did you hide your face from the Light of day?
Or did you say, "With you Lord, I can make it!"
Satan pounds us daily, O Yes, that is true!
But look up to the sky, and see God's brilliant blue.
Then get up and say with a smile on your face,
"Reposing awhile is not a disgrace."
You were beaten to earth, O, What a crack!

> **You didn't stay flat, so be thankful for that.**
> **The harder you're thrown the more glory for God**
> **When He changes your ugly scars into stars.**
> **So courage, Dear Brother, we have a battle to fight.**
> **With Christ as our Leader, we know we are right.**
> **Even though our eves are blackened with cares**
> **He holds the keys for our victory there.**
> **And even when brought to face death, what then?**
> **If we've tried to live life for the good of men.**
> **And with trust in our God we will hear our Savior say,**
> **"Beloved of My Father, I have missed you, ENTER IN."**
> **And eternally loosed from the tight fist of sin**
> **We WILL be home ever happy with Him!**
>
> *God bless you Jim, we are family, and family never stops loving one another – in good times and bad.*

After writing the poem, I fell asleep in my chair. When morning came, I had to tell Duane what had happened. As I predicted, Duane happily, at least somewhat I hoped, agreed that we would have to help Jim.

But, where do we start? After much discussion Duane stated that we had enough money to at least frame in an additional room. Jim needed our bedroom so we would have to make do. Sleeping on the floor was not a new thing to us. Actually Duane did even better than that for us. He bought a used queen sized couch and hide-a-bed. Isn't God good to help His children! Later he even found a used dining room set that we could use.

The day finally came when we drove to Tampa to pick up Jim at the Tampa train station. I was so excited I could barely contain myself. I was excited but kind of frightened as well. I have already related this reunion in a previous chapter, so I do not wish to be redundant, howbeit to say, I never expected to see my brother in such a state. I remembered Jim as a handsome 6'3" inch, 250 lb. man, but what I found was a wrinkled old man, barely able to walk. I wouldn't even have recognized Jim if his red hair wasn't sticking out of his hat, and he hadn't called me by name. He was skin and bone weighing no more than 140 lbs.

Jim had great difficulty walking. I didn't think he could make it to the car, but he did. His breathing was much compromised, but he had managed to make it to Zephyrhills, Florida, on his feet.

I was thrilled to see Jim, but I was very concerned about how I was ever going to manage and take care of him. Jim was totally worn out when we got home. We got him into our bed, and he fell asleep immediately.

After Duane and I ate a little supper, we made up our sofa bed to sleep for the night.

Jim slept well through the night, but I didn't. I thought that maybe it was because I was so stressed. I got up early to make breakfast. Jim got up early as well. He was hungry, but a little apprehensive because I had told him from now on he would be a vegetarian. Contrary to what Jim believed, he enjoyed breakfast immensely. I made freshly squeezed orange juice, decaf coffee, scrambled tofu, with onions and mushrooms, whole wheat bread, and vegetarian stripples (veggie bacon). Jim ate and ate until he could hold no more. I found out later that he basically ate one meal a day because he couldn't afford any more than that. My brother was basically starving. I determined that my first plan of action was to fatten Jim up and help him regain strength and muscle mass.

For approximately two weeks, Duane and I fed Jim sound nutrition. In between meals we hydrated his cells. In addition to all this we used colonic irrigation therapy and ozone therapy.

Jim decided that he needed to keep on with his natural therapies. He decided to move all of his personal effects and his truck to Florida.

He also had to break his apartment lease, but no matter; he was starting to feel stronger and he was gaining weight. Our children, Charles and Terri helped Jim move everything he owned to Florida. While they were doing that, we found a trailer park and mobile home near us that we moved Jim into. It was only 10 minutes away from our place. We barely moved Jim into his new place, when another problem reared its ugly head.

    I woke up in the middle of the night perspiring so much that my night gown and sheets were wet. I had an elevated fever, and I started vomiting. My abdomen was especially sore on the right side but the pain seemed to radiate sometimes to the left side. I was pretty sure from my symptoms that I was having an acute appendix attack. I was feeling really lousy, so Duane insisted that I go to the hospital. Sure enough, when I got to the hospital and endured all the tests and painful probing, I was told a surgeon was standing by for an immediate appendectomy. We learned my appendix was close to bursting. I was in the hospital for a day and a half and asked Duane to swing by Jim's place to see how he was doing. Imagine my horror when I found out that Jim was barely able to breath and turning blue. He was so ill; he couldn't even call out for help. I called 911 and requested an ambulance immediately. When the ambulance arrived, they asked me what hospital to take Jim. Two weeks before my hospital stay, we got Jim set up for all his needs at the Tampa Veterans Hospital. I told the EMTs to take Jim to the Tampa VA. The EMT called the VA and they refused to accept Jim; they said they were too full and they rerouted Jim to the Zephyrhills hospital where he had no records and no attending physician. I was furious, but Jim needed to get to any hospital quickly and be stabilized. I supposed that I would deal with the VA after Jim was stable. Little did I know, that Jim's hospital stay would be a month long and that he would almost die there?

CHAPTER ELEVEN

Remembering the Rehabilitation Experience & the Assault

Who could have believed that as I left the hospital from having surgery, that Jim would be admitted to the hospital, found nearly dead? The attending doctor, Dr. Ali, was very kind, but very guarded with what he told me. Basically he told me that he was doubtful that Jim would live through the night, and if by some miracle he did, he would need to have a spleenectomy immediately because it was strangling all the abdominal organs.

Well, Jim did live through the night and was stable again. Jim very reluctantly agreed to the surgery. Our daughter-in-law, Dr. Terry McEndree, helped Jim make that difficult decision. She knew the surgeon personally and highly recommended him. He consulted privately with me and told me his recommendations. I now had been given a power of attorney by Jim to make medical and other needful decisions. The surgeon told me with much compassion that he really believed that Jim would not make it through the surgery. I asked him to tell me what other option there was for Jim to continue to live. He told me that he knew none. I then responded, "What you are saying is that Jim might die sooner, or even today, if he has the surgery, but he will surely die without it. Is that correct?" He affirmed that it was correct. I remember saying, "Well, then, I think you must start the surgery." As he left me he assured me that he would do the best he could. I was in tears and shaking, but I believe I also asked him if I could pray for him and his surgical skills before he left the consultation room. The surgery lasted approximately three or four hours. I believe that before the procedure was completed, the surgeon informed me that Jim was still alive but he warned me that the most difficult time was now to come. He also cautioned me and tried to prepare me for what I would see as I was taken into the intensive care area to see Jim. I have never seen such a sight before. Lines and bottles of every shape and size were funneled into Jim's body, and he was unconscious. The nurses also warned me that they expected Jim to be unconscious for at least a few days and there was at least a 75% probability, that Jim would never recover consciousness. They also informed me that even though Jim was unconscious, he could probably hear me. They asked me to talk to him, read to him, and sing to him, and touch him just as if he were listening and talking back to me. For three and a half weeks I did this. Jim slept but kept breathing with the help of a breathing machine. I came every day to the hospital. Jim remained unconscious as read to him. Sometimes Duane, Terri or Charles spelled me and talked about the events of the day, the state of the world, and especially how good God was to us. Dr. Terri, our daughter in law who has a very large medical practice, came almost every day as well. She talked and sang to Jim in her beautiful soprano voice; she even shaved him and cut his hair and nails. Our son, Charles, came and talked and hugged and kissed Jim. Jim especially loved Charles and Charles reciprocated that love. I stayed most days as long as the hospital staff allowed me to stay. Even though I was once a professional singer, I think they grew tired of me singing almost every song in the SDA Church Hymnal. I also read to Jim most of the Gospels, Psalms, and Proverbs from the Bible. In many ways, as I prayed, sang and read from the Bible, even in this stressed and sad place, Jim and all of us were extremely blessed.

One day after Jim was given another blood transfusion, I thought I saw Jim's eyes flicker. I waited for another flicker, but it didn't come. Jim's hands were very badly bruised from all the needles, but I held it and shouted, "Jim, if you can feel and hear me, blink your eyes." I waited for, I don't know how long, but then he blinked. "Jim, Jim, I begged, open your eyes." And praise the Lord, he did! He tried to make a gurgling sound, but then went back to sleep. I was ecstatic! I knew that Jim was going to make it. Every day before I left his room, I would tell Jim to fight. "Keep fighting Jim, and don't give up," I'd plead, "you are going to make it, I know you are!" And I would leave him with a kiss.

From that day on Jim stayed awake for longer periods of time. Before Jim left the hospital the doctors performed a tracheotomy. Apparently because Jim had a breathing tube so long in his throat it damaged his vocal cords and crippled his swallowing responses. The doctors weren't sure that Jim could swallow or ever talk again because of so much bruising and trauma to the throat. For about three and one half weeks, Jim had been fed by an NG tube inserted into his stomach. Jim didn't care so much that he couldn't eat food, but he desperately wanted water. He would mouth the word water and make a cup sign with his hand. Of course Jim's body was being hydrated by another tube, but Jim wanted to drink. The doctors and nurses kept telling us that it was unsafe for Jim to have a glass of water because he still could not pass the swallowing test. They would give him ice chips, but no liquid water. The only thing I knew to do was to pray. Jim and I prayed that God would help him pass the swallowing test; about two weeks later he swallowed his first glass of water.

The next test to pass and endure was learning how to talk with the tracheotomy in his throat. He learned how to cap the trachea whenever he wanted to talk. Jim was a preacher so talking came easy to him. He not only talked but he sang with Terri and me thru his trachea tube. Jim was doing so well that the doctors decided that Jim should do the rest of his rehabilitation at a nursing home. Jim was excited that he could finally leave the hospital. He had been there for over a month.

The doctors convinced Jim that he could leave the hospital, but that everything that could be done for him had been done; it was now time to consider the obvious. They convinced the family and Jim that it was time for hospice care. They told us that Jim would be made comfortable at all times, but no intervention to save his life would be done. Jim agreed to go to hospice care. I was devastated. I was not prepared to give up.

The ambulance transported Jim from the hospital to the hospice center in Dade City. He had a beautiful room and caring nurses. But I was not resigned to give up.

Jim asked me to call his children and request that they come to Florida from New Hampshire to see him one last time and say goodbye. Jim had not seen his sons and daughter for almost twenty years and I really doubted if they would come. I talked to Jimmy Jr. by phone and gave the invitation. Jimmy was very happy to hear from me and said he would make all the arrangements. Actually Jim had talked to his sons when he first arrived in Florida; because I had pled with him to call them. Sara, his daughter, had not talked to her father and I knew she was very bitter toward her father about his abandonment of her when she was a baby. True to his word, Jimmy made all the arrangements and he, Sara, and her husband came for a weekend to see their Father.

It was a bitter-sweet reunion to say the least. As a result, a great deal of bitterness and pent up hostility was released. Jim bore up well under it, and he was awarded with hugs and "I love you", as a goodbye.

My family and I went to visit Jim almost every day. It was quite a bit further to travel to see Jim, but we would not consider not being there for him. I brought nutritional drinks, supplements, fruits, and good vegetarian entrees for him. I brought him inspirational music and CD's and when he asked for wine, even though I do not drink liquor, I even brought that for him. After all the Bible says "a little wine is good for the stomach."

An amazing thing was happening, Jim was growing stronger. He could even walk now with assistance. He asked me one day as I sat chatting with him, if anyone ever left hospice and went home recovered. I said that I believe that has happened. He turned to me and said, "That's going to happen for me too." Every day he seemed to grow stronger. Some of the staff actually got a little upset at me because I would not allow them to feed him their cuisine and especially their meat menu. I brought him fruit baskets and nutritional "smoothie" drinks. One day the social worker of the hospice center who had been trying to prepare me for Jim's death said to me, "I think you had better take your brother home. He is too well to remain here any longer." Then she added, with a smile, "I wish I had a loving and caring sister like you."

Duane and I knew that Jim, because of his trachea, needed more help than we could give him at home. So Charles, Duane, and I began searching for a nursing home in Zephyrhills that would take Jim with his extensive care needs. He could eat on his own now, but he was a full bed care patient. His tracheostomy care was very prodigious, well beyond any care that we could give him. He could not ambulate or walk on his own or do any of the ADL's (activities of daily living) without much assistance. Not only was he a full care patient, but Jim had no financial resources left. He was now a Medicare and Medicaid patient.

Finally we located a nursing home, where a friend of ours worked. This facility agreed to take Jim with all his needs. Everything went smoothly at first, but when Jim asked the doctor to be truthful about the length of his convalescence, Jim was not prepared for the answer. The doctor's response was that Jim would need rehab for at least a year. He plummeted into full scale depression. He did not want to talk to God, or even have me pray. Jim had finally hit bottom with his faith. He no longer believed that he was going to get better and leave that nursing home. He began to regress and grow weaker. One day when I arrived home late from shopping, I turned my answering machine on to find a frantic call from Jim that was made the night before. He was screaming, "Nancy come get me; she kicked me, please come!" Duane and I got to the nursing home in record time, to only find Jim frantic and very agitated. The nursing assistant that was helping him rather weakly indicated that an unfortunate incident had happened to Jim. As Jim began to relate to me what had happened, I could barely believe it. It seemed that the night before at the changing of the shift, Jim tried to reach something on his bedside stand, and he fell out of bed. When he fell he was so startled, that he had a bowel movement all over himself and on the floor. One of the women nursing assistants saw what happened. She was tired and wanted to go home. It was her responsibility to rescue Jim. She was so upset to see the mess and know that she had to clean it up that she swore at Jim and kicked him. I was appalled; I was more than angry; I was livid! No one was going to get away with doing that to my brother. I demanded to see the Director of Nurses. I really believe, even though she denied it, that she was aware of the incident. I demanded that a full investigation be done and that the police should be notified. The Nursing Director tried in vain to persuade me from reporting the incident. I not only demanded that it be reported to the police, but I also demanded that Jim be transported at the nursing home's expense to the hospital to see if any injury to Jim's frail body had occurred because of the therapists' assault. Jim finally settled down, he was safe once again.

Once again Jim found himself in the hospital. He was not alone. The police had followed Jim to the hospital where they were interrogated Jim about his recollection of the assault. Jim gave very clear and decisive answers to all their questions, but at the end of the interview, he refused to press charges. The police were not happy. They pushed him to press charges, but he would not do it. He said he refused to ruin a worker's reputation and profession over one ill-timed incident. The police officer tried to get me to reason with Jim. He argued that this might not have been the only time that the nursing assistant had done such a thing. Jim still prevailed that he was not going to be the patient that ruined her career. He would leave the results of that decision with God. Even though I disagreed with Jim's decision, he was trusting God again, and I was happy for that.

CHAPTER TWELVE

Remembering The Veteran's Hospital Experience & Senator Jenny Brown Waite

Jim's stay at the hospital was brief. Many of the nurses and therapists now knew Jim well and enjoyed talking with him. They admired Jim for his ability to laugh and sing, even though the tracheostomy, and bear up under so much pain. Our new dilemma to solve was to find a new nursing home that would admit Jim with his extensive needs and paying all the bills with Medicare. I had to give up Jim's trailer park home because it took his entire Medicare check less thirty- five dollars a month for personal items, to pay his nursing home bills.

We diligently began our search for a new nursing home. God blessed our efforts and it wasn't long before we had Jim placed safely in a new residence. The Director, Mary Ellen, was even a new member of our church. She reached out to Jim and gave him a lovely room and an extended bed to accommodate his 6'3" height. Jim loved the nursing home staff and they loved him right back. He even looked forward to his physical therapy every day. Before we knew it, Jim was walking on his own. One day, on a Sabbath, the whole family was in Jim's room having church. We were singing hymns and some of the nursing staff and a doctor came in and joined us for a while. Jim had been singing for some time with me through his tracheostomy. This always amazed the medical staff. Since Jim was a Pentecostal Pastor, he was in the process of giving a sermon to 'our' little congregation. After we had sung several songs the resident Chaplain came in to join us, he didn't realize that Jim was preaching, so he asked if he could have prayer for Jim. Jim smiled and said, "of course." After the Chaplain concluded his prayer for Jim, Jim asked the Pastor if he could take his hand. The Chaplain readily agreed; then Jim raised his right hand looking very lovingly into the Chaplain's eyes, and said, "My brother, why are you so troubled? You have not slept for days. Your family situation is going to turn out all right. Trust God, He is working everything out right for you." The Chaplain looked dumbfounded and could barely speak. "How did you know?" He asked Jim, "I've told nobody about this." "The Holy Spirit impressed me with this word of knowledge," was Jim's reply. The Chaplain heartily thanked Jim for this encouragement. He shook each of our hands and said as he departed from Jim's room, "I am going on to another patient's room now. Maybe I can be of help to someone else because I see the Holy Spirit has got the situation here under control." This kind of scenario happened time after time as Jim led patients, doctors, and nurses to the throne room of God. Hospital personnel, therapists, nurses, and even physicians, *(I will relate later about the experience of one doctor)* loved being in Jim's presence and having him pray for them.

Jim was growing stronger every day with the help of all the staff at this nursing home. Then one day as I was shopping at Wal-Mart, a call came on my cell phone. "Mrs. McEndree, this is Nurse Rice, Please come to the nursing home quickly. Your brother is in a bad way." Duane and I sped to the nursing home only to find Jim as red as a lobster and burning up with fever. I screamed for a nursing assistant and demanded that she bring me a large basin of ice. I'm afraid I wasn't to kind to her in my demands because I added, "And don't tell me you can't find ice, either, and bring it back immediately." While she went for the ice, I took all the wash cloths and towels I could find and soaked them in cold water in the sink. I pulled off all of Jim's clothes, and wrung out the towels and placed them carefully on his brow, neck and groin area. When the nurse came back with the ice, I kept wiping him down everywhere from the top of his head to the bottom of his feet. His temperature came down immediately from 105 degrees to 98 degrees. When I had Jim more stable, I demanded that Jim be transported to the hospital. When Jim was in route to the hospital, I asked the Director of Nurses what in the world happened. Why didn't they intervene for a therapy to cool Jim down and get him to the hospital? She very sadly said she could do nothing more than call me because they couldn't find Jim's doctor to obtain a doctor's order for treatment. I was disgusted and very upset with this reply.

As we arrived at the hospital I received another call. "Now what?" I wondered. I didn't have to wait long for the answer. The billing department wanted to see me. Jim's bill for his lengthy stay was approximately one million dollars. The breath almost departed from my lungs. And they informed me that the VA refused to pay any bills because Jim was not treated at the VA Hospital but at the Zephyrhills Hospital. Medicaid was contesting some of the hospital charges. I winced and groaned in my spirit as I looked heavenward and asked how I could even pay a tiny percent of the bill?

I was devastated by this news. I had to do something. I turned to God for counsel. With the Lord's leading, I decided to visit the VA and speak to someone in the business office.

Before going, I wanted to ask Jim what he knew about his veteran's administration benefits. It seems that he was awarded 100% medical coverage from the VA because he served in Korea on the DMZ perimeter during wartime. After further discussion with Jim I learned that he had helped the ROK soldiers administer a defoliant out of copper canisters that Jim believed was Agent Orange. This was a chemical that Jim helped spray on the trees and forestation so that the bombers had better sight to see the enemy as they bombed their targets. I began now to see why so much of Jim's cancer and medical problems were coming upon him. It was very apparent to me that Agent Orange had caused Jim's cancer. I began to learn how the progression of CLL was manifested in the human body, and researched all I could about Agent Orange and its relationship to leukemia. The more I researched, the more I was sure that Jim's exposure to Agent Orange caused his disease.

Before Duane and I left for my encounter with the VA officials, I was armed in my spirit. I had been warned by the local Dade City VA Advocate, that I would have a very difficult time getting any help for Jim even though he was entitled to it. How right he was! The VA spokesman turned Jim down for everything. They even questioned the fact that Jim had served in Korea at all; and especially if he was there while Agent Orange was being sprayed in the demilitarized zone. They denied that the VA had a responsibility to help Jim. Angry, I was much more than angry. I don't think I can pen a word for it. I think I even asked the uncooperative spokesman arbitrator if he slept well. He answered, "Very well, indeed." I looked straight in the eyes of that 'gentleman' and said sternly, "you don't even know WHO you are dealing with." Of course I didn't mean me. I really meant that he was dealing with GOD ALMIGHTY, and He can never fail.

When I got back home, I started writing letters. I wrote letters to our local newspaper; I wrote to FOX news; I wrote to Bill O'Reilly; and I wrote to Sean Hannity Report.

It was not more than a week and a half when I heard from Keith Caite, a local reporter from FOX news, that he had referred my letter to the Saint Petersburg's Time and a reporter there, Mr. Bill, who often did stories on the Veterans Administration. It wasn't long before I heard from Mr. Bill and he said that he was <u>very</u> interested in publishing a story about the VA's refusal to help Jim. He asked if he could come to the nursing home residence where Jim had returned to from the hospital and interview both Jim and myself. He also asked if the nursing home would give him permission to send a reporter out the next day to take a series of pictures of Jim and myself. We were delighted to say, YES, to all his requests.

The next morning, Jim and I were ready and waiting for the photographer. The photographer arrived early and took about fifty pictures of us from all directions. Jim and I could hardly believe what was happening. Then, the next day, Mr. Bill came to the nursing home for the story. I believe he spent about two hours talking with us and taking profuse notation. Finally our interview was over and Mr. Bill assured us that this was a good story for his newspaper. He told us it should be published by the following week, and he would call us and tell us when it would run. Mr. Bill's creditability was as good as gold. The next week he called and told us to look at the front page lead story of his newspaper. Jim and I could not believe what we were seeing; we just kept thanking him. Praise the Lord, we could barely believe it.

The very next day after the news story was printed, I got a call from the VA; I think the call came from the Director of the VA. The gist of the conversation was that he wanted to apologize for the way Jim was treated by the VA. He wanted me to understand that all veterans were treated well at the Tampa hospital. A terrible mistake had been made by a few people resulting in Jim's bad treatment. This was going to be rectified immediately. To begin with, he was awarded a fifty per cent disability pension; he would have all his medical bills to date, including the Zephyrhills Hospital bill, paid; he was to have assigned to him the best personal physician and oncologist they had to offer. He was to have a visiting nursing assistant come every day for his ADL's; a visiting nurse once a week to keep updated his medication. All of his medication and future medical stays at the VA and all the transportation needs for him and me were to be provided and paid for. The Medical Director asked me if I was satisfied with those arrangements. I answered, "Partially, but that we wouldn't be totally satisfied until Jim had 100% disability awarded to him for the life threatening condition he had sustained as a consequence of his service in Korea and his contact with Agent Orange". The director assured me that they would continue working toward that goal and said his good-bye to me.

Some days are just MEGA high life days and this was one! If that wasn't enough wonderful news, God rewarded us with some more. The phone rang again, and a federal secretary asked me to hold on while he put Senator Jinny Brown-Waite on the line. "Hello, Mrs. McEndree, this is Senator Jinny Brown-Waite, but please call me 'Jinny'. I understand that the Director of the Tampa VA has called you with some good news as I directed him to do just that after I read the news article in the Saint Petersburg Times." At last! I thought, I have the ear of someone who can do something for Jim! As I related from the beginning to the present time about Jim's plight, I am afraid I was getting louder and louder and more irritated. Senator Brown-Waite kept interrupting me with "Please don't yell at me". I continued with an apology but kept relating all the disappointments and noncooperation of the VA toward Jim. She told me that she served on the United States Board of Military

Affairs. I asked her if she understood the incompetence and unfairness of the VA toward the veterans and what was she prepared to do about it. She stated that the VA had just received more money from congress to meet the obligations of the VA for the veterans and the needs of their families. She assured me that she would be calling me again and would personally see Jim's case through to the end. Senator Jinny did call me on two more occasions, but she never did get Jim the 100% disability that he certainly deserved.

Jim, like many other American and Republic of Korean soldiers, died tragically and prematurely, because they were required to use and handle in service to their country the very toxic Agent Orange. To better facilitate battlefield tactics and win the war, this poisonous Agent Orange was used to defoliate the 'jungle like' vegetation of Korea.

For many years The United States Government, much to the sadness and hardships of American Veterans, refused to recognize the link to Agent Orange and accept the tragic ramifications that dying veterans were forced to suffer. This Government has <u>now</u> acknowledged that all military personnel exposed to Agent Orange while serving on the DMZ in Korea will be awarded 100% disability. It is believed by many health professionals to even have affected exposed veteran's offspring.

May God bless the many American voices and veteran's advocates that persevered and forced legislation to help these military heroes that gave the ultimate sacrifice for

God and country. THANK YOU FOR YOUR SERVICE!

CHAPTER THIRTEEN

Remembering the Last Two Happy Years

Jim was doing so well at the nursing home that it was decided the doctor would remove the tracheostomy cannula. The medical team decided that since Jim was to be treated from now on as a VA patient, he should come home to live with Duane and me. In preparation of that move, Jim had the tracheostomy cannula removed. At first it was hard for Jim to breathe because of the swelling, but with the help of the oxygen, he did just fine.

Jim was so happy to be home with Duane and me. Charles in his love and benevolence to Jim, bought a used mobile home for Jim that he had moved next door to our cottage. Now we had a little more breathing room.

For the most part, Jim was getting stronger and thriving. He went to the VA at least once a week for different therapies. Most of the time, the VA sent us by shuttle service to the hospital and back home again. Jim had gained fifty five pounds from the first time I saw him. As he stepped off the train he had weighed 146 pounds; he now weighed 201 pounds. I was rejoicing that Jim was being healed. Then one night Jim started having great difficulty breathing. Even with the oxygen, I noticed that Jim was in deep trouble. With much trepidation, I dialed 911. Soon the ambulance, a fire truck, and about 5 EMT's were at our door to take Jim once again to the hospital, but this time they took him to the VA Medical Center. The diagnosis this time was that Jim's blood and lymph nodes were full of thick blood and full of white blood cells. The cancer was raging again. The doctor's decision was to increase the Coumadin to a very high level but the scary downside to this decision, was that Jim could bleed to death without very careful monitoring.

I had to go into a VA office building to sign some admittance papers. When I returned to Jim's CR room, I saw a very frightening sight. Jim was hooked up to all kinds of monitors and transfusion and oxygen lines. I almost lost it as I viewed this horrible and disappointing sight. Jim, on the other hand, seemed to be in good spirits. The nurses and doctors, had somehow, stabilized his breathing and Jim, with the assistance of oxygen was breathing and talking normally. I noticed as I viewed all the machines and activities in Jim's room that he was speaking to a young VA medical lady intern. Again, I must ask forgiveness for not remembering names, because I just cannot recall her name, but I will never forget this doctor or this day. As I stood there, Jim asked if he might hold the doctor's hand. As he took her hand, he said, "Doctor you are such a caring physician, why are you throwing your life away on a man who continues to abuse you?" I remember her reaction to this day because the doctor started sobbing and loudly – right there in the ER room. "How did you know?" she sobbed, "I have told no one about my personal life." Jim smiled at her sweetly and said, "Sometimes my God gives me a personal word of knowledge when he wants me to minister to someone. Jesus Christ is very close to us now. You have a wonderful future ahead of you, Doctor. Our Lord does not want you to throw it all away. Do not give yourself to someone who is unworthy of you. Let's pray now and ask God to help you break away from Satan's man." I stood there almost hypnotized as I listened to Jim pray for his doctor. The doctor stopped crying, hugged and kissed Jim's cheek and promised that she believed every word of what Jim said. I do not believe that Jim ever saw her again, and I know that I never saw her again. As I have seen poets pen that some people are like ships that pass each other in the night, I believe in this particular case, Jim's cargo was the Holy Spirit.

I saw Jim share God's word of knowledge with many people. One day I walked over to Jim's trailer, soon after the visiting nurse had come for her weekly visit. As I opened the door, I found her on her knees and Jim setting in his recliner with his right hand raised and praying for her. Jim was leading her in the sinner's prayer to accept Jesus Christ as her personal Savior. After Jim had concluded his prayer for her, she turned to me and said, "God told me this morning that someone today was going to help change my life and show me how to be a Christian." Praise the Lord, what a Savior we serve!

As Jim lived at home every day with Duane and me, I don't think a day hardly went by that he didn't thank us for taking care of him. Even though he was dying, he knew through God's healing methods that we were buying him a little more time. He told Duane and me time and time again, that he had never been happier in his life than he was during this time.

A week or sometimes a little longer would go by, and Jim would have another trauma, and off we would go again by ambulance to the VA. Even now, I hate to hear the siren of an ambulance or emergency vehicle. It seemed that they were constantly being called to haul Jim off to the VA Hospital once again. The nurses and doctors in the ironic way were happy to see Jim. After they got him stabilized yet once again, he would pray for and with them. In many ways he would cheer them up as they made their numerous rounds. Jim hated to have me leave his hospital room to go home, but almost every day Duane and I would drive to Tampa to see him. When I went back to the hospital to see Jim, I would bring him a basket of goodies. Jim had no trouble in becoming a vegetarian because he loved my cooking and the many different entrees I made for him. He especially liked baked glazed Irish potatoes; stripples; lettuce and tomato sandwich; any homemade soup – especially pea soup; and chocolate éclairs. Once in a while he would ask me to make a marshmallow, peanut butter, and dill pickle sandwich like I used to make them for him when we were children because I thought they were 'pretty'. Even though Jim was hospitalized so often to be re-stabilized, he looked forward to those goodie bags, and so did some of the other veterans that were patients on his ward.

Our trips to the VA to see his doctor were memorable. His personal physician was exactly the right doctor for Jim. He has a wonderful laughing, dancing, happy eyes, and a great dry sense of humor. He was always encouraging and positive no matter what Jim's test reported. If one drug or therapy didn't seem to be working, he always seemed to have a plan B. His good humor always seemed to give Jim and me the impetus to keep fighting this plague. Another one of Jim's favorite people to see at the VA was his social worker, a raven haired beauty, as beautiful in her personhood as she was in her figure. She was a very good listener, and she seemed to enjoy Jim's inspirational talks. She tried and did help Jim and me walk around the many political and institutionalized road blocks that fabricate the huge Veterans Administration System.

I really believe that Jim fell in love with his social worker and I know that she highly admired Jim. Perhaps if Jim could have lived, she would have become one of our family. I really liked her and admired her so much.

As I have stated before, Jim was at the VA every week for something. Sometimes Duane drove Jim and me to the VA so we didn't need to take the shuttle. When that happened, look out, Jim and Duane capriciously enjoyed their wheel chair races. I, of course, was left in the dust. Duane was the horse and Jim was the jockey. They impenitently raced in the crowded VA parking lots and even when they felt it 'necessary' inside the corridors of the VA walls. They were like little boys again reliving their childhood. During this time Jim was really living a freedom that he had never had as a child. Jim and Duane had become good friends and buddies. Once in a while, I felt a little left out but I really didn't mind. I saw Jim really having fun – having fun in the midst of losing his quest for life.

During one of our weekly trips to see his personal physician, we were given the bad news. Jim's cancer had spread everywhere. He was still walking, at least, for short distances. His physician thought that it was time to talk to an oncologist. It was hard for Jim and me to admit that the cancer was gaining a foothold on us. According to what his doctor was advising, he seemed to believe that it was time to consider chemotherapy. Jim turned to me and with tears streaming down his face he reluctantly said that he thought his doctor was right. I disagreed because I am a naturopath, and I don't believe in chemotherapy at all at any time. Chemical therapy kills the immune system and when one has a weak immune system; it is like going into a gun battle without a gun. I loathed to admit that I had run out of options and therapies that we hadn't tried or tried that didn't work. Jim and I sadly took the elevator to the third floor to see the oncologist that his doctor had referred. When we finally got to see the oncologist, I must say I liked him. But I didn't like his prognosis or his therapies. I, of course, knew that Jim would decide the medical route he would take. Jim decided that he would begin aggressive chemotherapy the next week. I tried to be hopeful for Jim's sake, but I had very little hope for a therapy that I knew would poison the bodily immune system.

The following week Jim continued taking chemotherapy. It was a benumbing sight to see the long chemotherapy room with one long row of recliner chairs and men and women hooked up to chemotherapy bottles infusing into their veins. Jim was in good spirits as they hooked him up and I tried to lighten up and be as encouraging as I could. Jim was hungry because I gave him no breakfast. I thought that the chemotherapy might make him nauseous, and I thought it might be better if he didn't have food in his stomach to compound the issue. I went to the VA cafeteria to buy him a 'veggie' breakfast. All I could find there that wasn't meat and sugar was hash browns and whole wheat toast. As I entered the chemotherapy room with the scant breakfast in my hand, I found and heard Jim singing with and for some of the other patients. Since I was a singer as well, Jim insisted that I join in the impromptu chorus. One of the veterans told us to shut up. He said that this wasn't a happy place, and we were annoying him and everybody else. He got a cool reception from his outburst because everyone else wanted us to keep singing. In between the song singing, Jim would tell about the love of God and how he loved all of his children so much. He was so desperate to save each one of us that he sent His one and only Son to die on the wicked cross to pay the penalty for every one of our sins. Jim ate, sang, and sang all through his therapy, and he didn't get sick. Jim returned home and felt great all throughout the week. The next week we saw his doctor again to evaluate Jim's test and tell us the results of the chemotherapy. I was amazed and ecstatically happy, as was Jim, when he said Jim was in remission. The good trick he said was to keep him in remission. Imagine our bitter frustration and bafflement when we returned to the doctor's office before two weeks were up and found that Jim was right back at the stage he was before starting chemotherapy.

His doctor and Jim decided that they would try two more aggressive sessions of chemotherapy. I just shook my head and weakly smiled; after all it was Jim's decision. Within a month of Jim taking that last bout of chemotherapy, Jim died. He got weaker and weaker every day. The chemicals within his body not only killed the cancer cells, but it also killed his vital organs.

Jim lost his final battle in the war of cancer, but I know, I shall see him again on that sea of glass, because he was victorious through the blood of Jesus Christ. He will be healed and live throughout eternity forever and ever and even beyond that!

CHAPTER FOURTEEN

Remembering: Jim Falls Asleep

The early morning hours of Jim's death were for me surreal and blurred. I had fought so long and so hard to keep him alive that I found it unfathomable to accept that he was dying and slipping away from me. My blood pressure soared and I was in great physical as well as mental anguish.

I remember that Jim was taken to the VA hospital by ambulance yet again the morning before he died. Before I called the ambulance I went to Jim's motor home to check on him. I found him on the toilet unable to void and in pain. I immediately called 911. The paramedics rushed Jim to the VA and I stayed at home to gather up his personal effects, get dressed and ready for Duane and me to follow him to he hospital. We had a number of family issues that we were dealing with, so it took us a little longer getting to the VA than it normally did.

One hour or maybe two passed and I was still not ready to leave for Tampa. As I was completing my last chore, the phone rang. It was the intern doctor at the VA telling me to hurry to the hospital. Jim was dying, she said, and she didn't know how long he would hang on.

It was pouring rain outside and Duane and I tried to drive carefully and quickly through the downpour. Tampa is about 35 miles from Zephyrhills, and it was difficult making any time in the traffic and pouring rain.

We finally arrived at the VA and were ushered into ta ward where the terminal patients were treated. We were told that we had to wait while the nursing staff was putting clean clothes on Jim. Apparently, he had vomited. It seemed like we waited for hours. I know it wasn't, but it seemed as if it were. I wasn't prepared for what I saw. Jim was lying on the bed and his breathing was very shallow. I remember trying to talk with him, but he seemed unresponsive. At that point, I remember I started crying,, and told him how sorry I was for failing him. Dr. Terri McEndree, my daughter in law, had followed us to the VA. I had called her at her office before I left Zephyrhills. She took emergency leave to help me. I don't know what I would have done without Terri that day, evening, and early morning hours. Jim was hanging on and on much longer than anyone expected. I kept trying to talk to Jim but I remember not getting anything out that made sense. I was really hurting because of my extremely high blood pressure.

Terri and I sat down at the foot of Jim's bed. Duane could not be in the room because the medical staff only allowed two people to be in the room at one time. We all agreed that Terri was needed to interpret the medical condition of Jim and to help get me through the end of Jim's life.

As we sat there with Terri holding my hand and praying with me, all of a sudden, Jim sat up in bed and looked straight up. He had a wonderful look of peace on his face and a large smile. He was looking at something or his Healer. At first I thought that he was hurting or seizuring, but it wasn't that. Jim had a look of euphoria and reconciliation in his eyes, I kept saying, "What is it, Jim, what is it?"

He sat up for at least 30 seconds or more and then lay down on his bed again. He never answered my question. He just appeared to go to sleep, but he kept on breathing.

The pain from my hypertension was getting worse and worse. Terri said my face was red and so were my eyes. Jim was still hanging on. I talked to Jim's doctor and I heard myself saying, "I think I need to go home" "No", she said, "You need to stay here. He will be dead very soon." I couldn't take it anymore. So I approached my sleeping brother and said, "Jim, go to sleep, please, I need to go home and go to sleep too. I love you and I know we will be together soon. Terri is going to stay with you so that I can go home and get a little sleep." To my amazement, Jim shook his head yes. Terri understood my state and walked me to the door. "Don't worry, Mom, she said. "I'll stay here till the end, and then I'll call you." I had fought so hard to help save Jim. I couldn't stand it anymore. My head was throbbing, and I felt like I was deserting my dying brother. I actually think that if it hadn't been for Terri I would have died there that night as well. Terri made me understand that I had to leave; Jim's doctor made me feel like a deserter and a coward.

At three o'clock in the morning, Terri called me and said that it was all over. Jim had breathed his last and she was coming home.

According to Terri, Jim talked to her before he died. I don't know why he did not talk to me. He asked her to sing to him the hymn, "I'll Rise Again." Almost as soon as Terri finished singing the hymn, Jim breathed his last. Through Terri's song Jim had affirmed to God and all the unseen beings that by the saving grace and blood of Jesus Christ, He would live again and even for evermore.

CHAPTER FIFTEEN

Remembering Jim – My Concluding Thoughts

It is approximately five years after Jim's death, and I still find it difficult to forgive myself for not staying with Jim until he died. It seems, sometimes, unpardonable that I was not there when Jim took his last breath. I will forever be grateful to Terri for encouraging me to go home. I think that she could see that I was on the verge of experiencing a heart attack.

Jim, I believe, wanted me to go home. As I stepped out of the room, Jim went to sleep softly as he began to leave me and this world behind.

Some people might ask me, and rightfully so, why I would put myself through the anguish of reliving all the dysfunction of my family in this book. The answer to this question is twofold: #1. I wrote this book because I promised Jim I would do it. And #2. It was Jim's dying wish that he and I might help someone who has lived a selfish degenerate life understand that God is desperate to save them, and that He has work for them to do for Him that only they can do.

I remember reading from the Holy Bible and from a favorite author of mine that the "Brands plucked from the burning", are the very ones that are going to be closest to the Savior through- out all eternity. I know that Jim will be among that group and that he will be happy there. I love you Jim, I'll meet you in the New Jerusalem where we will never see suffering, abuse or death again.

DON'T QUIT

When things go wrong as they sometimes will,
When the road you're trudging seems all up hill,
When the funds are low and the debts are high
And you want to smile, but you have to sigh,
When care is pressing you down a bit,
Rest, if you must, but don't you quit.
Life is queer with its twists and turns,
As everyone of sometimes learns,
And many a failure turns about
When he might have won had he stuck it out:
Don't give up though the pace seems slow –
You may succeed with another blow.
Success is failure turned inside out-
The silver tint of the clouds of doubt,
And you never can tell how close you are,
It may be near when it seems so far:
So stick to the fight when you're hardest hit-
It's when things seem worst that you must not quit.
Gerifert 216